The Owner's Manual

The Owner's Manual

A Walk in Greatness

Pamela M. Young

Kingdom Living Publishing
Accokeek, Maryland

Cover design by TLH Designs, Chicago, IL
www.tlhdesigns.com

Published by Kingdom Living Publishing
P.O. Box 660
Accokeek, MD 20607

Printed in the United States of America.
ISBN 978-0-9968089-7-2

Acknowledgments

I thank God, my Lord and Savior, for introducing me to many processes, valley experiences, and people. They have allowed me, by the Holy Spirit, to expound upon His ministerial gifts of understanding and knowledge. I have learned to apply His precepts to my daily living. My life exemplary of faith has grown through perseverance, building patience, which is apparent, as my journey as a Christian needs continual molding. I humbly thank God for the Holy Spirit and counsel for revelatory knowledge that has changed my life. I am in awe of the power of God and His hand upon my life. Thank You for giving me strength no man gave, and no man can take away. I love You, Lord.

I thank my mother, Mrs. Edna M. Young-Coston. She is continuously an inspiration in my life in so many ways. I often say to myself that I would love to have the qualities she possesses to be a part of my disposition as well. She teaches when we are together. Often she has no idea how profound her statements are that reflect character. They resonate in my soul, a desire to be a better person. I hold these moments inside because they are precious, and I know that God sees the desires of my heart. He sees the portion I pray to incorporate in my life, as He is the Potter and I am the clay. Thank you, mother, for always being present for the journey of all your children and giving us memories that honor the legacy of the Young family unit. I pray God's choice blessings upon your life that you continue to have life and life more abundantly. I love you, mother!

In memory of my stepfather, the late Mr. Dewitt Coston. He was a strong and willed man and an example of a heart of compassion. The excellence of a man is not easily obtained, but the journey he took revealed the character that we saw. I am thankful to have experienced the company and support of such a man. Thank You, Papa-D!

I thank my sisters and brothers of the Young, Mitchell, and Coston dynamic. I am thankful to be the bridge that I may celebrate sixteen brothers and sisters who are intricately and distinctively set apart with brilliant gifts and talents, callings, and professions that cultivate our experiences. May we share with one another and with the world the seeds God has planted in each of us. Thank you all for being available for your destiny and sharing your lives with me. I love you all!

A special thanks to my brother Elder Darren Young for writing the foreword to *"The Owner's Manual: A Walk in Greatness."* It has been a journey unscripted that no one could have foreseen but by the grace of God and your stewardship. You have been a brother and man of God used to minister the Word in different seasons in my life. I thank God for your portion in my life, and a time such as this that we both can stand on the mountaintop. May the words in this book echo in the valley so that others are ministered to as well. Thank you, Darren. I love you.

Thank you, Ms. Laticia Fuller Lipscomb, a woman of resilience and courage, and my classmate of the Goldsboro High School class of 1990, for sharing your experiences in high school. May the readers be enlightened about how we all should treat others as we would like to be treated. Although your journey has been long and filled with many memories of particular times, Laticia, I agree that God has recognized your calling out the enemy who has used others and weakened his attempts as of this day. Because you have shared your story, it is no longer just yours but loosed so that others may understand they are not alone and that they can begin healing as well. We all are coming from somewhere; we just have to continue to take a step forward. Thank you, Laticia.

The Owner's Manual is written in memory of my father, the late Mr. William Alexander Mitchell, Sr. I am thankful for the memories I continue to hold true, knowing that God has a plan. May we all appreciate what is given and take nothing for granted. Each day is a blessing from above as we reverence God, who is sovereign in our lives. Rest in Heaven. I love you, Daddy

Contents

.

Foreword

David, who would become king of Israel, wrote most of the book of Psalms in the Bible. He was a shepherd before he became king. David had the ability to soothe and comfort others through music and words. However, he was often made uncomfortable himself through his many tests and trials. However, with the help of God, David was able to overcome them all and find comfort, strength, hope, and peace in his times of need.

Out of David's pain came wisdom, relationship, purpose, and ministry, to name a few; such is the case with Pamela Young. She has endured many tests, trials, and storms of life to come out better, stronger, and wiser.

Pamela is now in a place where she ministers hope, comfort, strength, and peace to those who will hear what she shares through words that paint pictures in our minds. Every word is a stroke of the painter's brush, making clearer the words she paints. She has a gift to bring words and pictures together. Pamela Young is the author of two other books, *"A Poet's Decree: Rhythm of Life* and *"Stand: An Autobiography of Poems for Daily Living."* She is a visionary and interpreter who writes about what she has experienced and sees, be it past, present, or, yes, even future. In the pages of this book, you will be enriched, encouraged, and inspired.

I have known Pamela Young all her life as she is the younger of my two sisters. I have seen her grow and mature through the storms of life. This book is therapeutic; it is like medicine and ministry. I know that you will find healing, comfort, hope, strength, and peace within the pages of this book.

Grace and peace unto you all.

Elder Darren Young

Introduction

Many years ago, when I was in the world doing what I wanted when I wanted, and how I wanted, God was communicating with me. However, I was too busy being selfish to see what was going on in my life. Surely, it rains on the just as well as the unjust.

> *But I say unto you, Love your enemies, bless them that curse you, do good to them that hate you, and pray for them which despitefully use you, and persecute you; That ye may be the children of your Father which is in heaven: for He maketh his sun to rise on the evil and on the good, and sendeth the rain on the just and on the unjust* (Matthew 5:44-45).

Romans 11:29 says, *"For the gifts and calling of God are without repentance."* To operate in the fullness of His gifts, we must give ourselves to Him so that He may show us who we are in Christ. Many are called, but few are chosen, and we must find our place in the body of Christ. After years of doing things my way, I decided to rededicate my life to the Lord.

I had begun to see where the Lord had brought me from. I was not aware of all the ways He had kept me safe from harm until He began to show me. Not only that, He allowed me to reference my past with learning and understanding times, places, circumstances, people, situations, and atmospheres that were established to destroy my life. He gave me a perspective so that I could be delivered from myself and healed to walk in my Godly inheritance. By the grace of God, I have been made available for Him to work in my life and use me as an instrument of His love, grace, and mercy.

I remember a dream I had many years ago: The hand of God extended from the sky, and He said, "I've come to take you home." I said, "I'm not ready to go." Later, I would experience a tumor in my womb, being diagnosed with sarcoidosis, then breast cancer. Those illnesses could have just as well taken me home, but God blocked it. I overcame by the grace of God, and it empowered my life. The experience makes the difference because it gives reference and an account that is the root of change. God enables us to choose faith and gives sight to our composition, which had not been shown or understood before the moments of distress.

Only God knows what we are made of; He wants us to know as well. I used to sit and wonder which way is the blessing coming from. I believe in miracles and that some miracles happen in an instant. I have been blessed to understand that God also warrants the experience as opposed to sitting, waiting, and believing. We must discover some things for ourselves, and only God can deliver us to our spiritual destiny.

I have experienced a journey that exposed me in retrospect that I may be empowered as well. Our miracles lie within knowledge and understanding, as well as the prospect. Therefore, be encouraged to take an active part in your miracles before the face of God. He will reveal yourself to you, exposing abundant and greater wealth in spiritual and physical health, a place where your miracles lie. So as you read *The "Owners' Manual: A Walk in Greatness,"* may you open your hearts to chance and change so that God may begin a new work in you. We all are pieces of each other's lives; we just have to find where we fit. I pray many blessings to my readers in Jesus's name. Amen.

Chapter 1

Separating Times You Feel
From Emotions You Own

Separating times you feel from the emotions you own references a ministry God used to deliver me out of a valley. The Rhema word encourages you to separate the times you feel, the spiritual impartations from His Word and inspiration, from the emotions you own. These are those emotions that occur when something happens or something has happened throughout your life when there is a trigger causing a learned behavior.

We are to stand for what we believe when spoken to and know the objective before the end, if possible. Observing someone without looking at them is to see them; know their spirit from yours, which bears the fruit you seek to try. There is nothing new under the sun. We are living in times where it is feasible to firmly discern one another and know the objective.

> *17Even so, every good tree bringeth forth good fruit, but a corrupt tree bringeth forth evil fruit. 18A good*

tree cannot bring forth evil fruit, neither can a corrupt tree bring forth good fruit. ¹⁹ Every tree that bringeth not forth good fruit is hewn down and cast into the fire. ²⁰ Wherefore by their fruits ye shall know them (Matthew 7:17-20).

There is no time for wasted time as children of God. Therefore, we as Christians have authority and power by His Word to discern spirits and be made aware of people and their intent. Words travel, and some spirits warrant no conversation; they travel from many people and are very strong, transcending generations.

Clever expressions are upon the faces of the wicked, painted beautifully with many colors and a refined demeanor and a heart that seeks to destroy. Compromise may be in your spirit; blind deceit will be cheap compared to the cost you pay for looking the other way. In efforts to see the good that does not exist, some find themselves in such a place. Because of the beauty that is in your heart, do not be deceived by what they can become. Only God has their completion, and it is their choice to seek Him. Shine as you are; they can see you as well and know the fruits that you bear. Either you will become their enemy, or they will become children of God. *The Lord is not slack concerning His promise, as some men count slackness; but is longsuffering to us-ward, not willing that any should perish, but that all should come to repentance* (2 Peter 3:9).

Do not be misled; at no cost is another worth causing your own embattlement that hinders your walk with God. *Do not give what is holy to the dogs; nor cast your pearls before swine, lest they trample them under their feet, and turn and tear you in pieces* (Matthew 7:6). Be careful as you approach the day, even more, when night arrives. The belly of the beast has many eyes and constantly seeks. Because people communicate like us, we give them dignity. Because they look like us, we give them humanity. Because they speak like us, we perceive to understand them, which makes talking very clever. During a time when I was seeking the companionship of others, a ministry from the Holy Spirit was, *"Don't suck from those who cannot blow in heart,"* which means not to seek to spiritually be fed from those who aren't capable of pouring into my spirit. Therefore, I was made aware of the boundaries about me, and they administered limits when it came to others.

It is wise to know your objective from the start and refrain from the lure of deception. Gird your mind with the Word of God hidden in your heart. These are the weapons of our warfare. Without them, we are unarmed and very vulnerable to the possibility of unbelief and a sense of ungodliness. They give off impressions of power, attracting your attention and awareness, thus opening the door for the power of persuasion.

The truth compared to love languages adhere to many different kinds. These include ones you want to be true (blind deceit), ones that conjugate the truth (amazing how telling the truth can also be a lie), and ones that are the truth. In either case, they give life to hearing and listening as well as receiving and deceiving. One must be able to identify what they hear that they may know whether to listen because once impartation begins, words become manifested and brought to life. *For as he thinketh in his heart, so is he: Eat and drink, saith he to thee; but his heart is not with thee* (Proverbs 23:7).

We must understand to discern the spirit of the conversation; not everyone who talks the truth has the same intent. The heart of an individual can make the truth a lie. O generation of vipers, how can ye, being evil, speak good things? *For out of the abundance of the heart, the mouth speaketh* (Matthew 12:34). Therefore, I encourage one to carefully assess and evaluate the messenger as well as the source. Although this is true, my motto is, "No one can deliver me as I can." One may deliver the message, but not with the heart; it may be said in a manner that destroys the entire message.

A man's belly shall be satisfied with the fruit of his mouth; and with the increase of his lips shall he be filled. Death and life are in the power of the tongue: and they that love it shall eat the fruit thereof (Proverbs 18:20- 21).

We should know our mental truths, as well. The enemy preys on the mind. Sometimes we are our own worst enemy. We have to know ourselves to a degree where we understand such thoughts are not feasible and becoming about who we are, calling the enemy out. As well, we need to know our self-defeating thoughts. We must know our mental truths. Wicked thoughts can nearly send a fervent Christian haywire. It happens, but we disengage the enemy's attacks by understanding who we are in Christ and know that the devil is the author of confusion. I have had thoughts and wondered where they come from, and right then and there is where I left them. They weren't a part of my heart's desire, nor did they agree with my spirit man.

An illness can plague the body without physical cause. Just thoughts and worrying are spirits of infirmity. The mind can make the body ache, have pains, become weak, and take away the desire. Merely by thought, we can experience spiritual illness no over-the-counter medicine or doctor's prescription can cure. When you know something to be true and allow oppressing spirits to torment the righteousness you exemplify in life by the Word of God and allow the spirit to make you physically sick and unstable, you allow the spirit of infirmity to manifest when there's no physical cause for such a thing. *Beloved, I wish above all things that thou mayest prosper and be in good health, even as thy soul prospereth* (3 John 1:2).

No matter what we are dealing with, His will for us is to have life and to have life more abundantly. So, in life, whatever you're dealing with, be sure to deal with it and not allow things to fester in your spirit that you won't become spiritually ill. Dealing with spirits of the mind that cause infirmities means giving them to God, not some but all. Some things are above the spirit of our head and are for our Maker to conclude. *"Spirits of the mind come in all kinds, jolting, provoking, sulking in tears as you grasp for spiritual humanity to keep your sanity."* This is an excerpt from a poem I wrote in *"A Poet's Decree: Rhythm of Life."* It epitomizes the places the enemy wants to take and abandon the children of God. This is why I reiterate how important a relationship with God is.

To recognize spirits of infirmity is to know God. I have experienced a spirit that weighed heavily on my soul. I could barely recall it to find my conclusion without it tormenting my body. I tried on several occasions to no avail. As I lie in bed, in the wee hours of the morning, God blessed me to understand that He has my completion. I had to trust in Him and believe what He's revealed to me in my daily walks with

Him. Ultimately, He has work for me to do for His kingdom. I had to let the things I was toiling with go to become available for Him. The spirit of infirmity is strongly associated with self-defeating thoughts.

Understanding what is taking place is the key. When I was a child, I sat at my mother's dinner table and thumbed through an encyclopedia. I came across a picture of the human anatomy and became very sick looking at it. The perception in my mind caused me to become sick. Therefore, I had to put the book away. There was no physical reason for what happened and no medicine I could take for it. Learning and understanding are powerful and bring deliverance.

Some people live with aches and pains that are attributes of the intangibles of the mind and are not aware of the cause. Self-awareness helps us identify our triggers and when they originated to help pinpoint the time of mental inception that plays a part in our physical oppressions. Again, I cannot tell you how important it is to establish a daily relationship with God.

It is impossible to break down a lifetime of the enemy seeking to destroy your life by yourself. There are things God will reveal to you that hold your deliverance. Then you will be made free and available for Kingdom work and your spiritual destiny as well. We often hear, "I'm going to take back what the enemy has stolen from me." We must understand and apply the knowledge to take back what the enemy has stolen; we must first go back to when he took it and know what he took. We must understand what spirits he imparted, the atmosphere, who was involved, the environment that revealed behavior, and habits that you've carried your entire life. Dismantling the strategy of the enemy is by the wisdom of God.

Again, when you make yourself available to God, He may take you on a journey through life to comfort the child whose voice was stolen by persuasion or whose innocence was taken by hatred, or whose mind was manipulated by tradition, or brainwashed by prejudice or cursed by generations. Despite a multitude of schemes meant for you to take to your grave, He will deliver on time. This is when you begin to heal and truly take back what the enemy has stolen from you. I am a living witness of this.

I describe my experience as a grown woman taking that twelve-year-old child in me by the hand and saying, "I love you; I'll speak up for you now that I understand. God has given me the knowledge to know and see what has taken place." Thus, I take back what the enemy had stolen and share with others that not only I may heal but open the door that others may journey through as well. And may they share their stories empowering others to live their lives to their fullest potential in Christ Jesus.

Sometimes people can be used as the source of the enemy's attacks early in a person's life. This may have a profound effect on their development into adulthood. This includes mischievousness, bullying with words that drop into one's spirit, and causing them to become depressed. This opens the door for the enemy and an onslaught of negativity to become a primary focus as days, even years, are the duration of this season.

With compassion and pride, I share the following story of a young lady who is very courageous in that she shared her experiences of being bullied in high school. The enemy's attempts are called out as she has gained strength throughout the years and now seeks God for her portion, her Deliverer, Healer, and Author of her completion.

"My Junior and High School Years"
by Laticia Fuller Lipscomb

My years in junior and high school seemed like the worst time of my life. I remember while I was in my science class, every day was the same thing: A guy picked at me. This was a constant struggle that I faced when I went to this class. On this day, he decided to take it up a notch, and I retaliated because I had enough. I took my science book and threw it at his head but missed it. I know that retaliation was not the answer, but it sure felt good.

Several years went by, and on to high school I went. Keep in my mind I was about 5'3" tall and had not matured any (no butt, no breast. I mean nothing). Every day in my classes, I was teased and tortured because of this. There were many days that I went home in tears only to have to endure the same torture again the next day. In my freshman year of high school, Physical Education class was a required course. That meant that I had to dress out in shorts or jogging pants, only to be tortured and tormented by my fellow classmates.

One day it got so bad that when I was on the bleachers talking to some of my friends, a guy came behind me and pulled my jogging pants down to my knees. He was never punished for this, and I had to return to this class every day after this incident. During my freshman year, it was never easy; I suffered every day from the torture of my fellow classmates. But during all this, I managed to keep my grades up.

I remember, like yesterday, one day in my sophomore year in high school, my mother bought me this satchel purse, and it had Egyptian symbols all over it. I took my purse to the gym and had to leave it in the locker room, only to return and find out that someone had stolen it and everything that was in it. Later that day, I saw two girls with it. I then went to the principal's office and reported it. I was told that there was nothing that they could do because I did not see them take it. In other words, it was my words against theirs.

I don't remember what year it was, but I remember the incident clearly. I was in my typing class, and a girl began to tease and torture me about my weight and my flat chest and no behind as she put it. This was an everyday thing for me to be tortured and teased by my fellow classmates.

I was so glad when I graduated from high school and put everything behind me. Still, I have never been able to shake everything that happened to me during my high school years. Now that I am a 49-year-old woman with three grown sons and three grandbabies, I still think about everything I endured during my high school years. Please know that bullying is real.

I remember well all the names of the people that made my life a living hell. When my children entered school, I refused to allow my children to endure what I endured in school. The hurts and pain that I endured in high school have haunted me to this day. When our 30-year reunion was held, I refused to go. I understand that people grow up and move on, but the torture and torment have lasted for years. When they say that KIDS ARE MEAN, I know; I experienced it my entire time in high school.

When the enemy tries to remind us to rewind and relive situations, it is a ploy to detain our thinking, which causes flurries of emotions. He wants nothing more than for us to continue to relive events and times in our lives when things were uncomfortable and adverse. The mind is the target of the enemy. His main objective is to obtain it. Therefore, we should keep our minds stayed on the things of God: *You will keep him in perfect peace, whose mind is stayed on You: because he trusts in You* (Isaiah 26:3).

We must know how to apply the intangibles—the things we cannot see—and understand the degree of separation. I understand through experience that the probability of my doing a thing is not likely, although I've not had the experience. My life's stat, if you will. The intangibles in our lives are as pertinent as the physical tallies we access and inform ourselves on and have confidence in ourselves about. They increase our faith so that we may fight a good fight as we run this race set before us. *For we wrestle not against flesh and blood, but against principalities, against powers, against the rulers of the darkness of this world, against spiritual wickedness in high places* (Ephesians 6:12). We must arm ourselves with the whole armor of God and the knowledge of His Word that we may appropriate things in life. *Study to shew thyself approved unto God, a workman that needeth not to be ashamed, rightly dividing the word of truth* (2 Timothy 2:15).

The intangibles or the unseen is a place that the enemy tries to mess with because there has not been an experience to warrant the physical lesson in life understood by the physical man. Therefore, we must trust the unknown's positive probability and not allow the enemy to confuse what has not taken place. It is a place that holds the lessons in life and nuggets of wisdom and revelations from God that confirm our affirmations concerning a situation.

It is like being healed instantly, receiving a miracle, believing, and having faith, opposed to being an active part of your miracle. Being an active part of your miracle warrants the experience to teach the life lesson. We must hold on to those things we know to be true.

There was a time when I was at my wit's end, and giving up was not an option. I constantly sought God. One day God allowed me to understand that I must go and do all I know to do and leave the rest to Him. When we stand on His Word when all else fails and crumbles around us, we will begin to see greatness. Imagine yourself standing on a rock in the midst of it all, trusting God; then, see yourself stepping down from that rock and being led by God. This is the life we live, the life of an advocate with the Father. Safe in His arms, where this world cannot do us any harm.

It is never over; we are always in the process. No matter where you are in a situation, there is an opportunity to capitalize and be even more productive. So, do not give up if you think you did not choose or decide when you should have. We stand in our change when we realize the continuation and that we are a work in progress. Acknowledging this allows one not to have a defeatist attitude or give up easily, assuming the deal is over. One more try, one more step, one more chance will make the difference. When you reach for the sky, know that the sky is not the limit because we are going there. Set your goals above and never beneath. A place where you may see there is more there to see.

Chapter 2

A Relationship with Christ

Jesus Christ came and died on the cross, rose on the third day, conquering death, hell, and the grave. He is the Rose of Sharon, the Lily of the Valley, the Bright and Morning Star, the Fairest of ten thousand to my soul, the Lamb, the Prince of Peace, the Everlasting Father, Jehovah Jireh our Provider, Jehovah Shalom the God of Peace, Jehovah Rapha the God who heals, El Shaddai God Almighty, the Alpha and Omega, the Beginning and the End, First and the Last, the I AM, Omnipotent, the Oneness of the Godhead, the Father, Son, and Holy Spirit, the Rock of Salvation, and as my grandfather called him, "Oh Master." An infinite list of names exemplifying His grace, power, and deeds, a legacy for His children to adhere to, and reverence, understanding greater works shall we do in His name. We are winners in Christ.

Jesus lived a life pleasing to God that He may appropriate things that presented itself in life and beyond. We share that same power to walk in His righteousness. We must apply the standards that Jesus exemplified to our own lives and experience His benevolence on the earth. Therefore, we have a portion of control. That is why we must learn to gird our thoughts.

As Jesus walked the earth, He died for us every day, resisting temptation as He was dead to sin, establishing a covenant that we may be redeemed by Him dying on the cross for our sins.

This reminds me of a young lady who came up to me and said, "You look good. What's going on, you pregnant, in love? Girl, you just glowing!" I raised my hand towards heaven and said, "You know what it is." She said, "Alright, it's God!" When we walk in Him, there's something about it that people will try to put their finger on, the peculiarity of the saints of God.

However, it should not be that we go to church and understand what the preacher is preaching, and not know when God is speaking. Some have a form of godliness but deny the power thereof that is spoken of in 2 Timothy 3:5 (KJV). He reigns outside the church doors as well. A relationship with Him has a daily sermon for you that separates you from routine, tradition, even more religion. Every day becomes Sunday, Monday through Saturday. You walk and speak with Jesus as He reveals increments of life and spiritual awareness. Sundays become a day when we don't forsake the assembling of the saints and a bonus in our Christian lifestyle, which is pertinent to the times in which we're living.

We are living in Egyptian times, where some possess the spirit of Pharaoh. Others have faith without works and un-belief in the power of God. There are Pharaohs in the land. People have reasoned, calculated, theorized the evolution of man, and voiced proof of the Creator's existence. Living for God, I quote them, "Is making life hard." Mankind and the range of freedom have allowed them to manipulate all truths concerning God. They cater to their own desires and emotions, freeing them from sacrifice, death of the flesh, and His righteousness.

It is saddening that such things are manifesting. But God will deliver just as He did in the days of Pharaoh's mystical, magical, intellectual attempts to match the incomparable power of God. His tongue ultimately cursed his own seed in an effort to stop God's prophecy. Again, God will deliver to all the Pharaohs in the land; therefore, we as Christians must be ready to be obedient when He calls as He did Moses. We are not obedient because they require proof, but because He is El Shaddai, God Almighty. Even then, some still may not believe and will drown literally in their own beliefs as Pharaoh and his army did. Just as He called Moses to cast his rod, so shall it be again. *For it is written, As I live, saith the Lord, every knee shall bow to Me, and every tongue shall confess God* (Romans 14:11).

Life is part of our physical and spiritual makeup, which completes the circumference of our being. We live the union of mind, body, soul, and spirit. *For the gifts and calling of God are without repentance* (Romans 11:29). Our gifts and talents indeed come from God. The physical, mental or intellectual concepts of truths are sufficient as well as the spiritual concepts of truths; they work hand in hand.

However, one has no extension of life, just the concept of truth. Adhering to the spiritual truths invites God in and is masterful in its continuation of the beginning and end of its fundamental truth. While scientists can come to a conclusion, God holds the end: *I am Alpha and Omega, the beginning and the ending, saith the Lord, which is, and which was, and which is to come, the Almighty* (Revelation 1:8).

Learning and being informed are great. But be sure to know the Master of the wind because He knows from whence it comes and where it ends, where the sea begins and where it ends, and ultimately has your completion. Some are being misled by their ability to understand; it is a gift from God. He gives completion in all His works in creation, but in Him lies the end. The Bible says, *"My people are destroyed for lack of knowledge: because thou hast rejected knowledge, I will also reject thee, that thou shalt be no priest to Me:*

seeing thou has forgotten the law of thy God, I will also forget thy children" (Hosea 4:6).

Ironically, the intellectual can be misled because some are too smart for the wisdom and knowledge that God renders, which results in a lack of understanding and being misinformed. Here is a rhema word ministered in communion with God: *"A snake can bite in many ways, one being the lack of knowledge."*

We Have a Choice

We have a controlling interest in the outcome when dealing with emotions. Applying the revelation *"Separate times you feel versus emotions you own"* is absolute. Times you feel are the spiritual attributes we know to be true—things you know in your Knower to be true of God. The emotions you own are behaviors that have occurred throughout your life when something happens or triggers a response.

However, we own universal emotions as human beings that have not been experienced that also give light to the truth. Jesus died on the cross for all our sins. Therefore, as human beings, we are capable of them all. We are saved by grace and are grace away from what we see and despise. Acknowledging these things should bring about a degree of humility and compassion when we consider ourselves in affiliation with others. Therefore, we should not judge one another directly or indirectly. Our opinions can have a judgmental stance even though we may not forthwith say you are this or you are that. We know our sarcasm and should refrain from such a degree as well and vice versa.

It is easy to become caught up when affiliating with people and caught off guard, so to speak. Therefore, we should pray without ceasing. There are many days when I constantly acknowledge God in what I am doing. If I am on the treadmill, I thank Him for my legs or that I am alive. If I am on the basketball court, I play hard because it is a talent that He gave me. If I am in a restaurant, I thank Him for grace. Praying without ceasing is being conscious and welcoming Him in our daily lives, which does not leave much room for the enemy's surprise attacks.

Although this is true, we choose what we answer to. If emotions say that you are inferior to others, it does not make you inferior unless you co-sign on those thoughts and believe it. We have the power to choose our stance regardless of the emotion imparted and perceptions of others. We can reject offense by applying a self-standard, which means despite receiving a negative connotation, find grounds of spiritual healing and sighting wisdom on the situation. This eliminates offense to your self-esteem because the battle is not yours; it is the Lord's. I am not concerned with intellectual textbook jargon and explanations as much as I am with the spirits they impart.

One day I encountered a lady and discerned she had a somewhat overpowering, condescending, manipulative sarcasm that she seemed to be comfortable with. She tried to impart what did not exist. Perhaps, because of preconceived ideas and labels, some choose to prejudice others. Who knows, but her words did not fit the desire that I am. Therefore, I rejected her words in my spirit and spoke accordingly. However, my words fell short of understanding, leaving the circumstance unattended to. Departure referenced in me the above, and closure in the spirit realm. Prayer found my end for the opposed and myself that the Word of God may ring true in my life and a stranger may be touched by the hand of God.

Replacing emotions with exemplifying the Word of God is key to living a more stress-free healthy life, something we should all aspire to. Being concerned with how to make ends meet in different arenas of life can be overwhelming. We should cast our cares on Him because He cares for us and not allow the cares of this world to choke the Word:

And these are they which are sown among thorns;
such as hear the Word, and the cares of this world,
and the deceitfulness of riches, and the lusts of other

things entering in, choke the Word, and it becometh unfruitful (Mark 4:18-19).

As we stand on His Word and believe in His promises, we know that His Word says, "I *have been young, and now am old; yet have I not seen the righteous forsaken, nor His seed begging bread"* (Psalm 37:25).

27 Which of you by taking thought can add one cubit unto his stature? 28 And why take ye thought for raiment? Consider the lilies of the field, how they grow; they toil not, neither do they spin: 29 And yet I say unto you, that even Solomon in all his glory was not arrayed like one of these. 30 Wherefore, if God so clothe the grass of the field, which to day is, and to morrow is cast into the oven, shall He not much more clothe you, O ye of little faith? 31 Therefore take no thought, saying, what shall we eat? or What shall we drink? or, wherewithal shall we be clothed? 32 (For after all these things do the Gentiles seek:) for your heavenly Father knoweth that ye have need of all these things. 33 But seek ye first the kingdom of God, and His righteousness; and all these things shall be added unto you (Matthew 6:27-33).

There are many ways the enemy tries to attack our minds and emotions, another being depression. I struggle with depression severely as a youth. In retrospect, the enemy saw me writing books and tried to destroy my mind, salvation, desire; you name it. For many years I fought a good fight for my livelihood and well-being. God revealed my purpose in life to me along the way. Now I may write unto the pages and empower others, applying this revelation: *Putting yourself in situations, regardless of how you think the outcome will be, and negative emotions are absolute in coming out of depression.* Experiencing events bring about change no matter how subtle it seems. The atmosphere, sounds, words, smells, images, and repressed happy emotions stimulate our subconscious until we are made aware of the subtle possibility of happiness again.

Do not allow yourself to be confined or withdrawn in your winter season; this is when God gives His greatest revelations. In those times, He wants to speak with you. We must desire to be made free from being oppressed as well as act upon the things we want to come to fruition. We are to abolish slavery of the mind that keeps us from growing and prospering in life. Faith without works is dead; we must fight a good fight with faith with works of perseverance and apply the revelation: *"Help begins with self, then the comfort of others."*

The wisdom and power of God are incomparable. I never thought in a million years that I would receive my life's revelation in part by an extension of a man who did not believe in God. For many years, I struggled with public speaking. I could not understand the immense pressure my body went through when the event occurred. I thought my behavior was just who I am, and that was it. Although this is true, it bothered me to be this way. I thought if I didn't have this hang-up, there are so many things I would like to do to inspire others.

My whole life, I have known myself to be brave and courageous, and I, for the most part, don't take any mess from anyone. However, what is this fear that keeps me on this side of the fence? I've never let it go. Deep in my soul, I've always wanted to know. What is this that has taunted me so? The Bible says, *"When wisdom entereth into thine heart and knowledge is pleasant unto thy soul; discretion will preserve thee; understanding will keep thee"* (Proverbs 2:10-11).

One characteristic I possess is competitiveness, and I remain determined to discover who I am in Christ. Therefore, on my own recognizance, I decided to step on the other side of the fence to do a television interview to promote my book. My objective was to know that I must trust God and see what awaits me.

In doing so, I realized I still was nervous but not as nervous as I perceived the day to be. Fear created situations in my mind that did not exist. My mind created so many episodes of what could happen, and none of them ever did. God gave me what I needed to do what needed to be done. And wisdom showed me the morning of the interview that I was on the other side of the fence. I was no longer contemplating what I wanted to do, but I was active in doing it.

It was a pleasure to my soul to feel God speak to my spirit. The Lord and I were on our way to do what I could not do by myself. When the interview was over and I returned home, I had such a feeling of accomplishment. I did something I didn't have to do, but I put myself out there anyway.

Later, I shared my experience with an individual who is in the business of promoting music and films and other events. He could relate to my experience in some fashion. We conversed for some time; however, his lasting question was, "Why do you get nervous?" My reply was, "I don't know," raising an eyebrow and slightly smiling. We made eye contact for about two seconds and resumed chatting about other things. Our conversations are always very interesting ones.

Remember, I said prior that God used a man that did not believe in Him as an avenue to impart wisdom and understanding into my life. Well, here is what happened. One day after exercising, I went into the restroom at the gym. As I meditated and washed my hands, looking into the mirror at myself, five words popped into my head, "Why do you get nervous?" I began to reflect on my childhood when my life changed forever.

The last time I had spoken with confidence was around the age of twelve. From that time on, I was told what to do and how I should be by the church I attended. The things I was told that I could and could not do had no bearing on my soul's salvation. I could not wear pants anymore, which meant I could not play my favorite sport. It bothered me, but I wanted to be obedient. Nor could I watch television and do a host of other things that separated me from everything, it seemed. I didn't completely understand. How could I? I was twelve. They were forms of religion practiced by the church I attended.

However, one afternoon after church, I ran home, changed my clothes, got my basketball, and headed for the basketball courts. Before I could get out of the yard, an adult stopped me and asked, "Where are you going?" I said, "To play basketball," and this person said, "You suppose to put God first." I replied, "I thought I just did!" The operative words here are, *I thought*. That was the last time I spoke my mind with no regard. From then on, I digressed and began to practice someone else's religion that killed a part of me that makes me who I am.

I associated speaking my mind with nervousness because when I did, it was impressed upon me what I wanted to do was wrong. Although I did not feel convicted inside, I did as I was told. I was dying on the inside and became very quiet as a youth. I wasn't persuaded by my own mind, and in all my learning, I didn't get understanding, which lowered my self-esteem and confidence. The developmental days of my youth were severely stunted.

Finally, I knew where this had come from. I had carried emotions impressed upon me at a young age into my adulthood. This was a very profound understanding to become aware of. I had longed for the summation to this question in my life. And I was in a place to receive a blessing. My soul rejoiced in understanding and knowing the source of the circumstance in my life and its origin. It prepared me for the fight to give a new response.

Many years ago, I rededicated my life to Christ. I recall experiencing what I call absolute silence. There were so many days that passed by that I had no communication with people. This reminded me of an excerpt from my book, *"Stand: An Autobiography of Poems for Daily Living:"* *"My thoughts were the company I never thought I'd keep. Again, after squirming in fits of myself, I am calmed by my Knower not to master the borders that have been laid."* One day as I sat on the porch, there was immense silence as I meditated. I told the Lord, "I surrender."

It was as if my ears dropped, and I could hear deeper. My insight became clearer, and I became closer to Him in the Spirit. I began to write even more things in clarity. The degree of separation may have seemed extreme, but the reason was as extreme. To reap obedience is to obtain incomparable wisdom unshaken and proved by God. During this time that spanned several years, I learned to really appreciate what I have and gave an account of doing so.

One day as my mother left my home, I watched her cross the parking lot, and the Holy Spirit rose up in me, and I began to speak in tongues as the Spirit of God gave me utterance. I thanked Him for her walk and grace that I may see her with such a piece of my heart to warrant praise. And so much more did I appreciate in my season of absolute silence. Separation from the things of the world and people holds salvation and deliverance. Embrace Him as He molds you right before the eyes of man into His completion. He has shaken the dirt from me and molded me unto this day. He lights the way that I may shine as sparkles are added to me daily. What God has for me is for me and what He has for you is for you. That is why I apply the revelation of the cause-gage, which means *there are times when someone else can stand; when no one can stand but you, answer the call.*

Often we wait to surrender our lives to the Lord because we figure our lifestyles are messed up. Before we do so, we want to fix it. I have one thing to say about that: It's not likely to happen that way. Ironically, that's the most common reason for procrastinating, obtaining eternal life. Before I rededicated my life to Christ, I remember being in places I knew were not good or conducive for me to grow in life. Deep inside, things did not add up. There was void and emptiness.

I remember praying one day, still indulging in a sinful way of living. "God, help me" was my cry as I looked up to the sky. I really meant it. It was as though I knew I couldn't transition from the place I was in by myself. Many strong realities took place in my life after this moment and in the lives of the people around me. God began to shake things up to bring about choices to be made and the opportunity to be set free. I believe He heard my cry, and ultimately, I chose Him.

You may be living in sin but know that God will and can pick you up from right where you are and begin to shake the dirt from you. One time I was at the bar in a club and began to speak of the things of God to the bar tender. Before the night was over, he replied, "You don't belong here." Deep inside, I knew this as well.

On a separate occasion, I told the Lord if He healed me, I would serve Him. My desire was to do what I promised. My situation was so prevalent that I didn't know how to begin. I never forsook my desire to serve Him or said I failed or denied my experience that day. I know God knew I couldn't find my own solution, but I desired to. As I reflect back to that time, I see how as time passed, He moved some things around so that I may see my way to Him. There is no orchestrated agenda that we take on our way to Christ. We just have to begin by receiving Him into our lives as our Savior, trusting that He will deliver.

I am so full of joy today because I know, *"If the Son, therefore, shall make free, ye shall be free indeed"* (John 8:36). I don't miss the things of this world and wouldn't trade them for my journey's end. I employ all who give ear to these sayings to be encouraged and inspire another. Trust God and experience something; until then, you've yet to have an experience. *Wherefore (as the Holy Ghost saith, today if ye will hear His voice, harden not your hearts; as in the provocation, in the day of temptation in the wilderness* (Hebrews 3:7-8). When you feel God calling you, answer the call.

The day I rededicated my life to Christ, I thought, "I'm going to trust Him to have my completion." I knew my lifestyle wasn't proof, nor was it tried and true. That is what God wants from us, to commit to Him and trust in His Word because He has our completion. Giving your life to Christ is like becoming a newborn all over again. Being born again, taking on Jesus' name, washed in the blood of the Lamb. Old things are passed away; all things become new.

As you begin to crawl and are transformed by the renewing of your mind—learning the ways of Christ and who you are in Him—the devil has already set up shop to deter your journey. When I gave my life to Christ, many contingencies were pulling at me. There was residue from the past, expressions, ideas, spirits, just a few of the enemy's tactics to deter my journey. I had no solutions for myself, so I said to the Lord, "Lord, I don't know the way, but I'm here; I need your help; show me how to live in this world." And He did.

If you are sincere in wanting to live your life for Him in truth, He will direct your path and not allow you to be a liar in Him. It doesn't take others telling you God's plan for your life or you feeding off someone else's experiences per se. Your own personal relationship with Him breaks barriers and invites unchangeable change no man gave and can take away.

As a Christian, God allows things to happen to strengthen your walk with Him, as well. Some time ago, I came down with the flu. I doctored on myself to no avail. Two weeks passed, and I decided to go to the doctor. After a week of antibiotics, I was up to par again. Three weeks in, I realized how relaxed my body had become. I had no aches, soreness, or pain from strenuous workouts. I hadn't moved this way in a long while. This is the way my body is supposed to move.

Grace allowed the experience that transformed my way of living, causing me to become aware of how to nourish my body effectively. "Another week away from the gym wouldn't hurt," I thought, just to make sure I was well enough in about five weeks. I was able to rest my body. Although I had often scheduled to have light workouts, it wasn't enough. I needed time away from the gym. It really resonated with me. Now I make sure I take at least two days out of the week to rest my body, sometimes even three.

Often the subtleties in life have the most significant impacts. To do the work God has prepared for us, we must be **able** to do it. We live the union of mind, body, soul, and spirit. We must nourish them all so that they thrive. Becoming ill gave birth to a blessing in my life.

May your words be known to you and applied in life, not just a rhythm of the mind that converses on cue. We must be the truths we speak in remembrance and in living, exemplifying our words with works of perseverance and faith. It is no good to know the Word of God and not know its power or experience it in life. That's like having a ship without a sail.

This reminds me of a passage in the Bible when the enemy spoke to the seven sons of Sceva, who wanted the power of God to do great works:

> *[11] And God wrought special miracles by the hands of Paul: [12] So that from his body were brought unto the sick handkerchiefs or aprons, and the diseases departed from them, and the evil spirits went out*

of them. ¹³ Then certain of the vagabond Jews, exorcists, took upon them to call over them which had evil spirits the name of the LORD Jesus, saying, We adjure you by Jesus whom Paul preacheth. ¹⁴ And there were seven sons of one Sceva, a Jew, and chief of the priests, which did so. ¹⁵ And the evil spirit answered and said Jesus I know, and Paul I know; but who are ye? (Acts 19: 11-15).

Do not allow yourself as a Christian to be foreign to the enemy because you do not have faith in what you speak. Get on board with your sail.

Ultimately, we are responsible for ourselves and how far we go in life. Sometimes we believe that some should be there to fill the gaps with support, a confidant if you will. At other times we acknowledge the people that say they love us are absentees. *"Don't worry nor fret if you're anything like me; these times will become stepping stones towards building a better you just as it did me"* (Stand: An Autobiography of Poems for Daily Living).

I recall October of 2005, after having a mastectomy of my right breast, searching for myself. I had hoped those I knew as my friends would render to me some normality, but it never came. What was I to do if I wasn't encouraged and lifted up by those with whom I spent countless hours laughing, drinking, smoking, clubbing, enjoying holidays, and numerous other events? Wow! Imagine pity patting around in your mind with that. They were just what they were and nothing more. Therefore, I had to reach inside, where many seeds lay dormant. Seeds waiting for life aspirations were watered so that I may begin to bloom, and my dilemma became a blessing. I knew that being secluded wasn't going to help, so I put myself in places to experience normalcy, if you will.

I remember being at a high school football game, sitting on the bleachers among strangers and acquaintances. I experienced emotions that brought a wonderful essence to the day. No one there knew what I had gone through, and it was like times before. I needed that somehow. In the end, I met a lady with whom I shared my life experience, what I'd been going through. She was ironically a wonderful confidant and seemed like a friend. I continued to move through life, allowing myself to experience new things and became more aware of who I am as I grew in life and in Christ.

As I sit here channeling myself back to a day and time when my life changed forever, I realize God's grace. The kind of cancer I had wasn't supposed to have bled, but it did; that is why it was found and diagnosed. My breast always had a clear discharge when I checked them. This one particular day, the discharge was brown, so I decided to get checked out. I was scheduled for a mammogram after being referred by my primary physician.

I will never forget the day I went in to get the mammogram. When the nurse placed my breast on the surface of the x-ray machine to compress it for the mammogram, blood discharged from my nipple, and I cried like a baby. My feelings were so hurt to see this happening to me. The nurse tried to reassure me that it didn't necessarily mean I had cancer, that it could be other things. I tried over the weekend not to worry, but it was the longest weekend I had ever had.

The following week I was called in to have a sonogram done, and it showed two masses in my breast that they wanted to biopsy. The biopsy results came back non-cancerous, but my mammogram came back abnormal. I had in carcinoma in my ductile area. The next week I was scheduled for a mastectomy of my right breast. The procedure was successful and a bit overwhelming.

Mentally, to retrieve what had been done was far from me. I think I was in a state of shock, seeing staples holding my chest together. There was no enunciation for what I felt. When my portion came to sorts, I was able to be released from the hospital. Until then, I had to stay. Looking at my chest caused me to become dizzy and lightheaded. My mother sat by my bedside. She watched her baby, the baby of six, begin the fight of her life, from the hospital bed to her house, where I started my healing.

To this day, I call her house, the house of refuge and healing. She has always been my support system. There was another who knew I might be in despair and wasn't there, one who knew of my pending diagnosis. Somehow, this empowered me even more to reach down deep for what I needed to survive and be vibrant.

Before the diagnosis of cancer, I went to the gym regularly and tried to eat well. The YMCA is my home away from home, so I was surprised when I became ill. But I learned a valuable life lesson. No matter what we do, sometimes things are just going to happen. At these times, we have to deal with what has been presented to us regardless of logic.

My mother told me, "Sometimes things happen; we just have to deal with them." I took her words and turned them around, saying to myself, "Sometimes things happen, just deal with it!" I taught myself mental toughness; this is how I encouraged myself. I also told myself, "No one wants to be around anyone depressed."

I learned to think about the things that were positive that I still possessed in life. When I became able, I walked around my mother's apartment complex, although I still had the drains in my chest. My mother wouldn't let me stay out too long. She would peek her head out of the door and say, "I think you should come in now Shug." I was determined to be restored.

I began to appreciate some of the non-support because it made me stronger and empowered me. I showed faith in God and leaned on Him, and He showed me who I am in Christ. We are so much and have so much to be discovered as a people. I received strength no man gave or can take away from me. When my body was through draining from my chest, the drains were taken out.

Later I was able to return to the YMCA. I remember being on the recumbent bike riding and thinking how things just seem to be going on as usual. No one in the gym knew what I had been through. Tears came to my eyes, and just as so many times before, right there, I could feel God saying, "I'm here." I peddled and thought, "I have one left breast and a sock filling the right side of my bra."

I was resilient and refused to allow the spirit of fear or illness to steal my joy and livelihood. The following month I opted to have my left breast removed. The cancer bled the first time, and there was a fifty percent chance it would come back in the left breast. When the pathology report came back on the left breast, it had formations that could have turned into cancer. Therefore, I was very comfortable with the choice I made.

I healed from surgery fairly well, recuperated at the house of refuge and healing with love only a mother can give. Afterward, I was diagnosed with lymphedema in my right arm from all the lymph nodes taken out to be tested for cancer, but that has not stopped me. In 2009 at the age of 38, I tried out for the Women's Elite semi-pro basketball team, proudly wearing my support sleeve.

In 2010, I published *"Stand: An Autobiography of Poems for Daily Living"* to encourage others to stand through the storms of life in the name of Jesus. My greatest desire is to live my life exemplary of my journey of perseverance and faith in God so that I can help others see they are not alone. I can share experiences that have molded me unto this day.

For those of us who find ourselves on common ground, may we lift one another up and encourage each other in life and in living. Always put your best foot forward and know if God be for you, He is more than this whole world against you.

The Author (#280) with 2009 Women's Semi-Pro
Basketball Coaches and Team at Tryouts

Chapter 3

Focused for the Journey

Often as we walk out our faith in God, we are made aware of the enemy's tactics. Having a relationship with God causes us to be able to discern by His Spirit when the enemy is roaming. We not only are aware of the orchestrated negativity, but we learn to give a supernatural response or reply when we're put in certain situations. Therefore, we thank God in all things because He works them out for our good. We become stronger, steadfast, and rooted in the wisdom of God.

As we journey in Christ and in life, there are levels where there's peace and no recognition of any disturbance, a happy medium, if you will. These are new places the enemy tries to invade. Because our adversary, the devil, is always trying to find a way to turn our peace into chaos, we must stay focused on the journey. It is rewarding to know that the old tricks do not work anymore, so he tries something else. This is a sign of growth. When your day has gone well, and the most subtle thing is not supposed to disrupt the day, but it does, that is the work of the beast.

I learned this one day when a man talked to me as rudely as he could because I disagreed with him. I watched him as he strutted around, throwing his weight, voicing where I stood on his premises. Finally, he told me to leave without my belongings. I was totally taken aback, but knowledge and wisdom spoke for me:

> *A good man out of the good treasure of his heart*
> *bringeth forth that which is good, and an evil man*
> *out of the evil treasure of his heart bringeth forth*
> *that which is evil: for of the abundance of the heart,*
> *his mouth speaketh (Luke 6:45).*

I told him I wasn't leaving without my things and that he was rude and would have to answer for how he talked to me. I said that I was going to pray about what happened and that he would learn his lesson. And that he may not learn it from me but from someone else. I meant every word I said, and strangely enough, he somewhat paused and agreed with me but persisted in his rude way. Perhaps to minister some resolve my way, one of his employees noted to me that he has a problem with his temper.

Later, when I returned home, I realized how I had grown in life. I did not challenge him as he challenged me. When I prayed for him, I prayed for his soul salvation as well. I even asked God to forgive me if I did anything I shouldn't have. So, the enemy may step into your growth only to grow you even more as you choose righteousness instead of a mess.

Remember, in a previous passage, I said, "I don't take any mess from anyone?" Well, I don't. There is a way to handle all things, and we must choose what is good. Although this is true, I was tempted and tried to the extreme but was grounded enough in what I live and believe that the nasty spirit could not enter my spirit. I did not respond on the same level as the opposed. I saw this divide even amid things. This is the power of God that reigns true. That is why we must pray without ceasing and meditate on the things of God. As I stated earlier, we do this to not be caught off guard by the enemy's attacks and taken somewhere we don't want to go.

In life, there are times when it is feasible to remove yourself from a place, person, or environment all together because the strength it takes to abstain from a thing is absent. Rather than trying to resist an apparent temptation and its contingencies, removing yourself would be a better approach. For example, I live a life of healthy eating habits. If I bring a box of Little Debbie cakes and soda into my house, I will eat and drink until they are gone. That is why I don't do so.

One Friday, I purchased some snacks for a friend and her child so that I could offer them some treats when they visited me. Days passed, and they had not been to visit me. I called to let my friend know I bought some things for them because she knows I don't keep certain snacks in my house.

After about four days, I became more conscious of the snacks and was tempted to have some. I finally broke down and had not just a portion but more than I should have. Because I associated sweets with being unhealthy, emotionally, that became my state of mind. Before long, it was Friday again, and no guest had arrived. I decided that it was time to get rid of the snacks because they were defeating my purpose, and the idea of them hovered all the time. Once I made up my mind to give the snacks to the kids in my neighborhood, their influence on my mind left. Just knowing they were in the house altered my thinking.

When we are around something or someone who can influence our decisions away from a positive perspective, it becomes a conflict of interest. It may prove that we are better off to ourselves. The same is true with being around someone that is unproductive and negative; just their presence brings a state of mind even before any possible temptation.

The very elect can also become the source of the enemy's attacks. Some practice religion and Christianity but do not allow their teachings to empower their lives. Therefore, they are powerless to the enemy's use of their lives and perpetuate the same spirit of weakness even inside the church doors. When the spirits of the saints begin to steal your joy, there is a problem. So, do not be misled by people that occupy the church house in their own might rather than God's strength.

I speak with a humbled spirit, but I am invested in you to call it like it is. We are in a constant battle as Christians, and it is okay to break free of those who do not walk the walk. Recognizing such situations are the defining moments in our lives. How we choose to handle circumstances makes us—building character that strengthens us not to be retaken in that manner.

Teach them in the church. The schedule an individual keeps is certain. Sometimes there are those who do not have a church home or had one but are no longer affiliated with it. However, God is always with us and often allows His children to encounter one another in the wilderness of life. We receive nuggets and confirmation from one another to inspire us even more.

Constant visits to the church allow the body to keep time and perpetuate a routine that delivers unto the flesh a cycle. The idea of the church can become preconceived and manufactured. However, we must stay focused and remember the reasons for fellowship so that we are not caught up in the routine. We come into the house of the Lord with thanksgiving and to praise and worship Him.

As we walk daily with God and our relationship grows, we will encounter other Christians outside the church. They are a part of edifying the body of Christ, and we often receive spiritual confirmations from God. Whether in the wilderness or outside of the church doors, there is prophetic placement. Just as the fourth man walked in the fiery furnace with Shadrach, Meshach, and Abednego, an angel shut the mouth of the lions to protect Daniel when he was thrown into their den, and an angel appeared unto Joseph to reassure him about marrying Mary, the mother of Jesus, may we experience the awesome power of heaven and walk closer to God. *Verily, Verily I say unto you, He that believeth on Me, the works that I do shall he do also; and greater works than these shall he do; because I go unto My Father* (John 14:12).

As we journey forward, we must be careful in our learning as well as understanding because what we assume to believe is what we become. There are truths laced with deception as its original meaning goes out the door upon delivery. I once began reading a book that quoted the Bible. Some interesting points warranted a further read, but my spirit would not allow me to receive what I had read even though it held the truths of the Bible. Those truths were for my attentiveness to subtly introduce the other writings. It was orchestrated very carefully to manipulate the mind. But God will not allow such a thing when you are truly rooted in Him.

I found myself for several days in limbo because my spirit would not let it in, although it was a very interesting concept on life and spirituality. I always want to grow and learn more, challenging the area of my circumference. Because of this desire, faith moved me in the direction I should go with understanding and awareness. It was a place I had not been aware of before.

As I stood in this new place, I realized the revelation of my thoughts spoken many times over, "God will not allow you to be a liar in Him. He is the Truth and the Light. So, in all our ways, we must acknowledge Him, and He will direct our path. Everything we need is inside us as we trust in the Holy Spirit, our Comforter and guide.

In the book of Luke, the devil tried to tempt Jesus with the Word of God:

> *⁹And he brought Him to Jerusalem, and set Him on a pinnacle of the temple, and said unto Him, if thou be the Son of God, cast thyself down from hence; ¹⁰ For it is written, He shall give His angels charge over thee, to keep thee: ¹¹ And in their hands they shall bear thee up, lest at any time thou dash thy foot against a stone. ¹² And Jesus answering said unto him, It is said, Thou shalt not tempt the Lord thy God* (Luke 4:9-12).

So even though someone may quote the Word of God, even in your reading, it can also be used improperly.

I realize that we must be careful of the information we choose to receive and inform others of as well. Some information has no merit and is very well associated with talk instead of speaking, which accredits reference and revelations. *But avoid irreverent babble, for it will lead people into more and more ungodliness* (2 Timothy 2:6 ESV). When we can give an account of our experiences, there is moral credibility to say a thing. Otherwise, one may not know what they are speaking of. Some transfer information and have no understanding of what they are saying. Others seem to just have a habit of saying whatever comes to mind.

However, these are realms the enemy operates in as well. When we choose to spread a word, we should be sure it is worth the delivery. Words are very powerful and very well may cause more harm than good. I have found that some people just like to talk profusely. *Do you see a man who is hasty in his words? There is more hope for a fool than for him* (Proverbs 29: 20 ESV).

One day I was approached by a man with a question that challenged my mind. His spirit was nonchalant, and he had an aura of passing the time. His spirit was not of God or divine. After discerning as much, I declined to receive his words. I told him if what he wanted to say wasn't going to encourage me to do good; then he was wasting his time and mine. He smiled as if to know that what I had said was true and managed to blurt out what he was thinking.

His question warranted no further thought or repetition. I identified it as trickery and an attempt to cause confusion. It was a prime example of why we must continuously pray without ceasing so that we may not be caught off guard and taken some place we assume not to be mentally or physically.

As light and subtle as they may be, even things we hear are apparent in our psyche. So be careful of the noise you choose to be present in whether you have chosen to extend yourself to listen. Sounds are clear, and your cognitive mind is aware. Have you ever been doing something, and a word came out of your mouth that someone else says all the time, and you wondered why you just said it? Well, it is because of heavy association.

Sometimes even though we choose not to listen to someone, their constant repetition conditions our minds to a thing. Therefore, we must be cautious of our surroundings as well. Prime examples are commercials. We don't try and learn the words to them. They show them so much our minds pick the words up, and before long, we know the commercial without effort. Words people impress upon us are very powerful indeed.

I am sure we've all had someone tell us about someone before we even met them. Whether the picture they painted was positive or negative, when we finally meet or see this person, the first thing that pops into our heads is what was told to us about them because a seed was planted in our minds. Although we know not to judge one another, that opinion is apparent. Therefore, we should pray that God will gird our steps as well as our minds so that we may be covered and walk righteously in His wisdom.

One day, I encountered a man whose words displayed previous concepts of thoughts that gave me the notion that I should stay and listen to what he was saying. Although we both entered the store to make a purchase, there was more that we both received from one another as we began to have a conversation. We stood for some time, conveying and listening to one another.

I smiled, and he knew I was on the same page as I understood some things he spoke about life. Then, my Knower inside made me aware that there was more being said as I continued to stand there. So, I listened for what was good, even if it sounded bad. Because sometimes, we have to go through something to obtain what we never had.

He spoke of relationships, married men in the church, married women outside the church, the reasons why people are so quick to have someone in their lives, and all that they will sacrifice—a woman to have a man and a man to have a wife. "There once was a married couple. The wife said her husband worked all the time; he was a workaholic. Don't you know if that man really loved that woman, he would find time to be with her," he said as I stared into his eyes, interested in what he was conveying. "That man worked all the time because he didn't want to be around his wife; the job was his scapegoat. People get married for the wrong reasons and stay married for the same.

A woman will have a man because she thinks she's getting old and too much time has passed by, or she thinks she should be married by now. She'll have a man even if she's not in love with him just so she won't be alone." He spoke as though these words were spilling out of him in verse so much so that I asked, "Are you speaking from personal experience?" He replied, "Yes, I've lived and seen some things in my life." He continued as he spoke of a man he knew who was unhappy in his marriage. But he didn't want to get a divorce because he didn't want to lose what he had worked his whole life for, and his wife felt the same way. So, he and his wife decided to stay together and continued to be unhappy with one another, living in a nice home and driving nice cars. To everyone else, they looked like they were living the life. But behind closed doors, they slept in separate beds and barely spoke to one another.

He spoke of another couple that he had observed in a restaurant. He watched the man get up and get some lemonade and didn't ask the woman if she wanted any. When the waiter came to their table, he asked the woman if she wanted more to drink, and she said yes. They sat there and ate, not saying a word to one another. When they were done, the man looked at the bill and got up from the table, and began to leave. The woman followed behind him.

"Some people will put up with this type of behavior for the duration of their marriage, even until death. When they go to the graveyard, they holler and cry and carry on. When they return to the house, they're calm as can be, wondering why they didn't die sooner," said the observer.

"Do you think a thirty-year-old woman and a fifty-year-old man's relationship will survive?" As I paused in thought, he answered his own question. "It'll work for a little while; after some time, the man will become more like a father figure and will become controlling. He will try and keep her away from her family and friends. People make choices like the music of today, sounds real good, but have no meaning."

He spoke of long ago when women knew their husbands were cheating or were gamblers or alcoholics. "When the man got off work, the wife treated him like a king, and he walked around the house like so. But the woman knew what she needed to do to keep the house running and kids taken care of. She made sure to get to her husband before he would go out and spend all his money on the mistress, or gambling, or drinking."

So much information, and I chose not to let it hit the floor. The hard truth of the matter is that these are someone's experiences, and they have impacted an individual who, by no mistake, chose to share his portion. I'm confident in my spirit that these words are meant for someone who read this book. In perfect time, learning will become understanding, and God's grace will abide in your life. As the Spirit of God travels to make way, may you be present.

Oh, how the irony of the days seems to coincide with moments in time. To the tune of four days, I encountered another man who seemed adamant to release his portion as well. It couldn't be a coincidence, I thought, as the multitude of information poured from his lips without question. Early one Saturday morning, I saw a familiar face, one I had not seen in a while. However, I obliged a dear old friend. As we sat down and he began to talk, I saw it was a business call. After he'd given me a description of what he was seeking, the conversation took a turn. And I stood at an about-face to him.

Wow! His life began to spill from his lips like water from a fountain. At first, it seemed like too much information. I heard the ins and outs of nonsense, wasted time, and selfishness until my spirit was quickened, and God allowed me to see its significance.

Then I began to listen and receive understanding. My friend mentioned several different women he had dealings with and a few he still dealt with. He spoke highly about God and praised Him. From our conversation, I gathered that he sold alcoholic drinks from his home, but only to a select few. "But I don't run a liquor house, though," he said. "Sometimes, I might even drink a beer with my company and listen to music." He also mentioned a ploy where he lied to keep one woman at bay, using another as the scapegoat.

As I sat there hearing these things, I wondered if he could hear himself as well. Further into the spilling, he said that he knows he doesn't do everything right, but he just asks God to help him. He seemed to put God in his life where He fit. As he talked, I could see that he really believed in the sincerity of the wrong he was doing. His demeanor was indicative of this, as he showed no remorse as he told stories of his life.

As Christians, we can't do everything others do; otherwise, they can't see the difference in us. What will make them want to receive Christ if we are no different from them?

He also wondered why women seem to take advantage of his nice ways. Well, I thought, if you came to them when they are vulnerable dangling what they need in front of their faces, their natural human behavior would be to obtain what they need. Their state of mind is focused on one thing, getting what they need while you are trying to find favor by preying on their vulnerability. Do not expect someone with tunnel vision to be able to see you while you have hunted them.

Because we are professing God, there is a banner as Christians we should carry that separates and distinguishes us from the rest of the world so that we may not camouflage ourselves with others' behavior and like environments. Granted, we all have our struggles, but we should never use them as excuses to do wrong.

I often am aware of the position I must take. To take it is to embrace humility and grace that only God can give. There are times when we are set in a place to just listen. It's Saturday again, and wouldn't you know I received a phone call. My dear friend wanted to meet again. He finally arrived at my home, and we sat and talked for hours about life, relationships, of course, and ultimately the Lord.

He spoke in-depth about a few things that concerned him and mentioned some things that I found in my spirit to address with the Word of God. I didn't know whether or not he could hear or see himself in his situation. Sometimes when we are in a thing, it is hard to see ourselves. I previously read in Scriptures, *"Reprove not a scorner, lest he hates thee: rebuke a wise man, and he will love thee"* (Proverbs 8:9).

Likewise, God provided the spew from his lips to open the door perfectly for my entry. I obliged the passageway as I began speaking the sentiments of my heart, and he received what I'd been led to share with him. He knew the things he had been doing were not appropriate for a Christian and, in his words, "wrong." He said, "When I lay down at night, I say, "Lord, I know this is wrong."

What God had encouraged me to say to him was confirmation to shake things up a bit. Although I had seen my dear friend several times since his first visit, it was not the time to speak to him about the things he had been doing. When God clears the way, you will know it is your time to speak; until then, be patient and diligent in Christ Jesus. *He layeth up sound wisdom for the righteous: he is a buckler to them that walk uprightly. He keepeth the paths of judgment and preserveth the way of His saints* (Proverbs 2:7-8).

Sometimes the lessons we learn in life are not just our own; and may take place in the presence of many, which can bring about a great deal of humility and submissiveness. It is also a prelude to maturation and growth upon your will to righteously come from a place. If you can receive an open rebuke, you will be able to receive open praise by many, as well.

There are times when God gives us confirmation of the spiritual ambitions of our hearts. One morning as I sat in my car drinking coffee, my treat for the day, I watched an elderly woman walk to the dumpster. She appeared peaceful and vulnerable as well. To her vulnerability, I wondered if she knew the Lord. I even thought to go to her and be a witness, but I was not sure it was the time. My mind said, "Now is the time because I don't know what tomorrow will bring." When I motioned to get out of my car, she had already gone into her house. For days she stayed on my heart.

One day as I sat on the porch with my mother, the little old lady went to the dumpster again. This time when she left, she began to walk towards my mother and me. She stood on the porch admiring my plants. It turns out she has a green thumb and thought I was doing something right with my plants. After discussing the different ways we cared for them, I learned that she knew my oldest brother as she engaged in a conversation with my mother. She often went to my brother's shop and told him to close on Sundays and go to church. As some time passed, we got to know one another, and I learned that she is a Christian. God had revealed to me the spiritual ambitions of my heart and that she is indeed a child of God.

Life's Leading Lessons

There once was a billionaire who owned many businesses. One day his son came to him with an idea. He said, "Dad, why don't you open a business and let me run it?" His dad said okay. "Wow," his son said, "why didn't you open a business for me to run, to begin with?" The father said, "You have to find your own way, son."

Even though the silver spoon was apparent, there are still lessons to instill. We may be blessed with certain things, but we must not enable our loved ones not to reach for their potential. Giving them what should be earned deprives them of warranted appreciation, instilled humility, and a proper perspective on life. Our heavenly Father owns cattle on a thousand hills, and they are all ours to claim, but we must claim them in His Holy name.

Stay faithful to Him and do your part as well. Revelation knowledge says, *"Don't 'eggo your faith; once you have it, don't let it go!"* See, God begins to bless you through your experience. *"I hope the job won't be the thing that eclipses anyone who has a crush on life."* Our objective must be productive in all aspects of getting. May we be sustained in prosperity and the righteousness of God by His plan for our life's abundance. Being prayerful and watchful is contingent upon the maintenance of our spiritual continuity in Christ. May we be elevated to higher heights, conquering measures big and small.

There were two friends, and one friend made better choices in two different situations. So, the one friend said to the other, "You've outlived me twice." The other friend said, "The only way I can outlive you is you are dead." The opportunity to make a better decision is always apparent. Do not ever give up. This was a very productive encounter between friends.

Often, people seem to recall the event or wrongdoing of others. They keep a record, if you will, of wrongdoing. Although an individual may have lived a long life evident of righteousness in Christ, some constantly remember their past mistakes. Apparent in life, we come short of the glory of the Lord. When we fall, the most important step is to get back up. Sometimes in our attempt to stand, we are pressed down by others. They stand as well, speaking in repetitive renditions of that thing that caused you to fall in the first place. Therefore, I apply the revelation, *"Don't remember as you should, but as you must."*

Love is patient; love is kind. It does not envy, it does not boast, it is not proud. It does not dishonor others, it is not self-seeking, it is not easily angered, it keeps no records of wrongs (1 Corinthians 13:4-5).

There seems to always be someone who remembers when. But I declare that some may keep you in their minds a certain way, but it is your portion not to stay.

"Let the good leg bear peace with it when the dirty one becomes withered." Whatever has become a hindrance to you, whether physical, mental, or spiritual, do all that you can to press forward. And when you have done all you can, stand on His Word. Continue to seek Him for revelation and peace no man gave, and no man can take away.

"Here now find now after," whatever the situation appears to be, you will not fully know all it entails until you explore it. Do not ever let anything stop your continuation. No matter what the circumstances or how bad something

may hurt at the time, right where you stand is the beginning of overcoming what tried to destroy you. When we are hurt, it seems as though we can't move, and life will stop right then and there. But I assure you there is more to come if you challenge yourself in the process.

A broken heart can steal your life and livelihood, especially the betrayal of someone you thought to be a keeper of your heart. Even then, abundant life is waiting for you! It may be hard to grasp at the time, just always know God has a greater will for your life. Challenge yourself to believe in His Word when it is showtime. *"I was slain, so the enemy thought; my reign was over, but it was mandatory that I got up."* Stand and allow your presence to tell the story and behavior to be indicative of who you are.

Speak blessings into your life. *Once you say it out loud for others to hear, it's loose then. Death and life are in the power of the tongue: and they that love it shall eat the fruit thereof* (Proverbs 18:21). Therefore, we manifest our victory through what we speak. *To everything, there is a season.* Time will bring everything into its proper place. Be sure not to allow your emotions to keep you bound after your season has ended. We choose what we answer to and have the power to reject emotions and replace negative thoughts with what the Word of God says.

Humility Before God

If my people, which are called by my name, shall humble themselves, and pray, and seek my face, and turn from their wicked ways; then will I hear from heaven, and will forgive their sin, and will heal their land (2 Chronicles 7:14).

We have to make time for our spiritual growth. Sometimes we get so caught up with the day-to-day that we fail to feed our spirit man. I recall many days where I sat on the porch, and God revealed things to me day in and day out. As time progressed and I began to share His blessings with others, I found myself drained and in need of spiritual filling. I thought I would quiet myself and sit on the porch where I'd received many blessings from the Lord. Something wasn't the same as I sat there wondering what it was. I was hungry and needed to be fed.

I journeyed on with a conscious mind knowing my need. God blessed me to understand that I shouldn't be tradition-al, habitual, or maybe even pretentious, thinking that He will bless me in a certain place. Thinking that way would be trying to contain Him. I understand that He is omnipotent, and just because I do not experience Him a certain way does not mean He's not there.

Later, as I continued to seek Him, I awoke one morn-ing, and my spirit felt a oneness with the words, seek Him.

There was a presence that my spirit understood that spoke and calmed my inner man. I felt that God acknowledged my efforts, and I should continue to seek Him. This meant that I was to look for Him to receive a blessing every place I go. We cannot get caught up in traditional rituals that contain and bind us into bondage and set boundaries. Sometimes we're at fault; other times, we can be subject to behavior transcending generations.

One evening as I attended a community gathering, I was blessed to see a perception of generational oppression. Once you acknowledge and have the wisdom to combat certain inadequacies, then it becomes your generational oppression. If you choose to do nothing about it, once enlightened, it becomes your children's responsibility and then your children's children, if not adhered to. I saw a meeting hall filled with people whose behaviorisms seemed identical to one another.

Therefore, I am certain to make others aware of sleepwalking and conjugating with cousins, friends, and even enemies. This oppressive generational behavior subtly settles in those lives whose presence has a loss of enlightenment and awareness of a productive mindset and an avenue to build upon. It sets up shop for all who inhabits its presence. When we are in a situation, it is very hard to see its makeup. By the grace of God, our desires are made available so that we may grow in Him and in life.

Now I know how to stand by His Spirit, and my posture in the Lord rebukes negative spirits. Being in His presence reproves darkness and manifests light. Perhaps these spirits that taunted me were about a generation of people and a race that began in my life long ago. However, perpetuated in the neighborhood I grew up in, they are negativisms that were taught and impart certain spirits and spiritual behavior. They lie and have said in many different formations, "I am the tail and not the head, beneath and not above." These spirits manifest themselves in a look, an exposure, or appearance that conjugates itself amongst its peers. They are seen amongst relatives and friends until someone finds out and these spirits are identified.

Now heads are straightened, shoulders are lifted, and eyes can see, forming a gentle rebuke to the person or persons, even a generation. The light must shine for them to see what you once were and that you are saved by grace. Children, mothers and fathers, and friends await understanding, guidance, and love because they have been told a lie.

Having a true relationship with God can bring a person from such a place, giving them full awareness of what is taking place so that they may be made free. Some circumstances in our lives must be dealt with for us to come from a place. Only God has the increments of your life to satisfy all that you need.

Free from the Past, Mindsets, Emotions, and Conscience

1. We are molded by circumstances that are conquered by faith

2. The Holy Spirit renews the mind and cleanses the heart

3. We are free from past sins and wrong mindsets

4. God molds past emotions, behavior, and responses

5. We are called out by the Holy Spirit

6. The new creation sees the calling out

7. The Holy Spirit indwelt causes us to see

8. Our hearts are remorseful

9. We want nothing less than a clean heart

There may be times when it seems that God is not there, and so much is going on in your life that He has forsaken you. Remember His Word: *I have been young, and now am old, yet I have not seen the righteous forsaken, nor His seed begging bread"* (Psalm 37:25).

And about the ninth hour, Jesus cried with a loud voice, saying, Eli, Eli, lama sabachthani? That is to say, My God, my God, why have you forsaken me (Matthew 27:46)?

Jesus experienced what felt like God had forsaken Him. But God has allowed me to understand we have to use what we know as much as we know, even when it does not seem like it, feel like it, or look like things are getting better. God will honor our forward steps. The reward is great to believe in Him through our circumstances.

Jesus reaped eternal life, resurrecting from the dead, sitting on the right hand of God, and atoning for our sins. One day the dead in Christ will rise, and those that are alive and remain will be caught up to meet Him in the air. There we will receive eternal life in heaven and dwell with the Lord forever. So, we must carry on and fight a good fight of faith so that we may someday hear Him say, "Well done, thou good and faithful servant."

Therefore, we should aspire for the best, be a light to others, and lead accordingly. As a true leader, one obligation is to lead no matter whose emotions are aroused to the left or right. Whether friendships, loved ones, enemies, no one is to stand in the way of the truth. As a child, I remember reading a piece of paper my sister had pinned on the wall. It said, "Stand for something, or you'll fall for anything." Those words stayed with me throughout life, and I have found them to be of great purpose.

Associating with people who do not represent what you stand for is detrimental to your leadership and can taint your name. Nothing is worse than that. *A good name is rather to be chosen than great riches, and loving favour rather than silver and gold* (Proverbs 22:1).

Association can brand a person even if they are not indulging in sin or a sinful act. Rest assured, when this happens, your acquaintances are trying to figure out the best way for them to get out of a bad situation. If you are truly rooted in Christ, this will become a stepping-stone. For example, let us say you were charged with a crime. Knowledge and wisdom will be the guides that lead you out of the courthouse with no charge because of favor. Before becoming saved, you were charged with a crime and could not be released. However, your friends left the building—free to go—and promised to come back for you, but never did.

The officer looking over your paperwork realizes the charges you incurred are now obsolete and argues your case. Soon after you receive the good news, you are released and free to go. Wouldn't you know, the first persons you run into are those friends who did the disappearing act and promised to come back for you. They stand with the same mischief upon their lips.

Here is where you look into their eyes and let them go out of your life and begin to experience *dept freedom; it may go all the way around, but it's coming back to you. No matter how long it takes, what you put in is coming out. It is profitable that we continuously sow good seeds so that we owe no one.* In this case, it is crucial to be a leader rather than a follower.

However, one must know how to follow to be an effective leader. To understand the needs of others, sometimes we must stand in their shoes, creating the experience. We must know when to lead and when to follow.

Must I belong to a church to be a leader? Anyone can be a leader, but to be an effective leader, we must line up with the Word of God:

The mouths of the righteous speaketh wisdom, and his tongue talketh of judgment. The law of his God is in his heart; none of his steps shall slide (Psalm 37:30-31).

[14] How then shall they call on Him in whom they have not believed? And how shall they believe in Him of whom they have not heard? And how shall they hear without a preacher? [15] And how shall they preach, except they be sent? As it is written, How beautiful are the feet of them that preach the gospel of peace, and bring glad tidings of good things (Romans 10:14-15).

Attending church is conducive to spiritual growth in life and in Christ. Studying the Word and fellowshipping with others help us become effective leaders inside and outside of the organization of the church: *Not forsaking the assembling of ourselves together, as the manner of some is; but exhorting one another: and so much the more, as ye see the day approaching* (Hebrews 10: 25).

Although I may not walk with my nose to the sky with pride, there are degrees of separation concerning my person that needs attending to, needs to die if you will. Jesus died for us every day as He walked the earth resisting temptation so that we may be redeemed. And He died on the cross so that we may have eternal life, establishing a covenant for us and an advocate with the Father. He took the journey we must take as we walk the earth and resist temptation. When we walk in Him, there is something about it that people will try to put their finger on, the peculiarity of the saints of God.

One day as I stood at a gas station about to put gas in my car, a young lady that I've known for some time came up to me and said, "You look good. What's going on, you pregnant, in love? Girl, you're just glowing." I raised my hands towards heaven and said, "You know what it is." She said, "Alright, it's God!"

I recall a story about a very promiscuous guy who selfishly ran around with different women. He often met up with the guys to play basketball, passing the day. Some of his so-called friends nicknamed him 'below the diaphragm Cunningham.' This was by no means an accolade but a label to set him apart from the rest and, at times to cast shame from members of the group who respected their wives and relationships.

Cunningham was a tough cookie to crumble as they taunted and teased him about true manhood that the others exemplified. He brushed them off, hinting that he was living the life. Deep down, he knew the truth and the emptiness he carried. Before long, life happened, and the guys didn't see Cunningham for months.

Then one weekend, when they gathered to play basketball, there was Cunningham. He looked the same as usual but they noticed a subtle difference about him. Instead of his old temperamental loud self, he was just the opposite, quite calm, to be exact. The guys just had to know what was up with him, so they asked. Cunningham looked around at the guys and said, "I have a son, and his mother and I have moved in together. I'm trying to make a better life for my son now." The guys couldn't believe he had it in him to settle down and take responsibility this way.

It all sounded pretty cool except for their cohabitation, thought one of the guys. So, he sat down and shared the Word of God with Cunningham. "That's wonderful you're stepping up with the mother of your child. What would make everything perfect is Jesus in your life. Also, your son needs to know who Jesus is. It's your responsibility as a parent to raise your child up in the way he should go, and when he's older, he'll not depart from it." Cunningham listened intensely and agreed. Therefore, as we journey in life and in Christ, we all may not arrive at the same time, but our job as Christians is to be a vessel that others may arrive as well.

Chapter 4

A New Inheritance

I speak to many people who reference their genetic make-up—the illness that plagued their family from generation to generation. I pray that it won't become their fate. I encourage them to understand that we become new creatures in Christ when we become saved and confess our sins. Old things are passed away, and all things become new. We are washed in the blood of the Lamb and have been bought with a price. We then are the bride and He is the groom that will one day return and establish in us perfection. Therefore, we have a new inheritance in Jesus Christ. We are to speak life and cast our cares upon Him because He cares for us.

> *But ye are a chosen generation, a royal priesthood, an holy nation, a peculiar people; that ye should shew forth the praises of Him who hath called you out of darkness into His marvelous light* (1 Peter 2:9).

While we labor in Christ and await His return, we are heirs to the inheritance of all the promises of His Holy Word. *Therefore I say unto you, What things soever ye desire, when ye pray, believe that ye receive them, and ye shall have them* (Mark 11:24). We must believe the Word of God and not what statistics say. We are to have faith in the positive outcome of the unknown and not allow worry to creep in and still our joy.

Do not allow anyone to cause you to waver in your beliefs to the point you become double-minded and confused: *A double-minded man is unstable in all his ways* (James 1: 8). I believe when you begin to doubt God, things He has blessed you through start to become unraveled as your perspective changes. When we believe our behavior reflects our thoughts; that is why we visualize the ball going into the basket before the shot. It is having faith in the unseen: *Now faith is the substance of things hoped for, the evidence of things not seen* (Hebrews 11:1).

A Powerful Perspective

Life becomes frustrating because we bring about our own concepts through negative thinking. It is not about the emotions we exhibit and rationalize but the true Word of God. The bottom line is to have faith and perseverance.

"Trust in the LORD with all thine heart; and lean not unto thine own understanding. In all thy ways acknowledge Him, and He shall direct thy paths" (Proverbs 3:5-6).

When we are not mentally prepared, trying to make a move in a certain direction may cause more harm than good, not just for you but also for others involved. Acting on impulse can be costly. When you jump into something, you may find the staying power overwhelms all those around you and becomes time-consuming. Although this may be true, some may lend a helping hand from the sentiments of their heart. The efforts of others may not be as inviting. So, when you find yourself in a sticky situation brought about by haste, take the time to evaluate the decision you have made that got you there. Then embrace the lesson life teaches.

Landing in the mud can help you live a more sanitary life and show you who your friends are. Some people may give an extra effort at their expense and others to gain expense. Both are noted for their intent and deeds, as they are observed with a seeing-eye that hasn't been revealed to either of them but to the individual who tries the fruit of the Spirit.

Sometimes the path we take may not be as apparent as we would have it to be. We may have to rely on faith and the experience of another who has taken the journey. Although this is true, our destination is prominent. God uses those He loves as His instruments to empower others in their walk as we run the race that is before us. At such times the Holy Spirit will be our guide and reveal whose hand to grab hold to.

Sometimes life's journey would have us tread water, run steps, or force a fall to outrun the enemy. Exemplify diligence when primarily you cannot see an opening. There may be someone else who can effectively make a move. The *cause-gage* is indicative, so make the call. Sometimes our ideas and creations may become an extension of someone designed for that moment to fulfill its completion. We all are pieces of each other's lives; we just need to find where we fit. However, sometimes we fight for things that have become obsolete. Be sure to focus your time and energy on a solid moral objective that has staying power. When things crumble around you, you will know what you are standing for.

The journey in life may have its bumps and bruises as you stand about-face to your protégé who has found success and extends a hand to give you a check, a payment due at their expense. Nevertheless, it is right on time to pay some bills.

As life unwinds, you look around to see where the money should go, the broken window or torn boards on the floor. Before you know it the money is spent, even though the protégé was heaven sent. Bless God when there is little and when there is a lot. You will remember where you come from.

The self-righteous, boastful, and arrogant ways of others will be why some will not accept or appreciate what is owed to them. Sometimes others are careless with money because they do not know the value of what they have or what it took to obtain it. What one person does not appreciate, another person will. And their denial becomes someone else's gain that catapults them to their next level. All things become a stepping stone if we choose to take the step, just as we make lemonade out of the lemons that life hands to us.

There may be times when the game is on the line, and you drop the ball because you just cannot get in the proper position. These times are stepping-stones as well because others are watching. Some will criticize; others will criticize and have the compassion to help. Always assess and evaluate what is being said and look forward to your next step. No one can keep you from taking it but you. *The brand you use may not be the best to insert for quality that your end result will be pro. Sometimes the recipes call for pure butter to obtain the rich taste you seek.*

We all make mistakes; when we do, some soul searching is the most important thing to do. Look for your next step and be obedient to His Word. *Because someone comes to your meeting doesn't mean they're for you; in fact, they may just as well vote against you.* Things are not always the way they appear to be, even concerning others. However, in either regard, it is an opportunity to ask God, "What can I learn from this?" It is always the right moment to capitalize on any circumstance.

I believe God wants us to not become complacent in our run. We should not think because we are saved; we have arrived at the point that we stop running. He allows our experiences in Him to fuel the fire of faith and perseverance. No matter what the test is, know that it is to grow you in life and in Christ.

There once was a man whose wife found him in a fetal position crying like a baby, and she murmured, "I hate a man who torments." The pain was so unbearable he could barely stand to his feet as he towered above her and suddenly began to speak. "In these sorrowful times, my own wife tortures me." He said. "How can I win, O Lord, when I have to fight Satan and man?"

Sometimes the very one who says they love you are out of sight many days, leaving you with the biggest fight of your life. Rest assured, the victory will be sweet. Just as you lay with your face to your feet, you will stand once again, defeating Satan and towering over man.

I presumed at once the concept of babble but was made aware of it as I sat near a man who, after a few words, realized we knew the same person. Before long, he blurted out, "He's sick; he don't take his medicine like he suppose to!" With no regard, he spoke as if his words had no power and that he knew all there is to know about this other person. I said, "What?" He said, "He's sick!" The spirit that was attached to his words was awful. I could only imagine the many people who speak into the lives of others and are not informed of their sayings.

Because I knew this person and knew better than his propaganda, I said, "He's been diagnosed with an illness; he's not sick." I do not believe in perpetuating negativity and certainly not as he was proposing. He calmed his spirit and got on board. We should speak things as though they are, not to be disillusioned but faithful.

I realize the multitude of people who perhaps have the same mentality. There may be those who sit and chatter about what your end will be—a universal babble perpetuated by man and a mentality that has not found God's righteous ways. Even from a distance, it is your portion to bind the spirits in the air from where you sit. Rebuking and casting down words that travel to their maker is our portion while fighting spiritual warfare.

When we become aware, power unfolds peace and freedom. Often in our lowest moment like our brother Job experienced, people can desperately disappoint us. Because our refuge is in God, it is our only strength and all we need to stand once again. We must remember who we are in Christ. And allow Him to deliver by His consolation and salvation, which becomes our ministry and a testimony to others.

Chapter 5

The Light of Behavior

Sometimes people may avoid you because of their mischief, even when an obvious hello would be the proper and normal action. However, their shadiness will find them out as they maneuver to keep cover. The honesty of those who are not in the plan may reveal their other hand.

There is nothing wrong with calling it like it is to avoid partaking in time wasted. One may become vexed at the idea of you doing so. Still, the outcome will be a valuable lesson for onlookers as you choose to pray for the individual in question.

As a car cover is placed over a car to maneuver the rain, so are the ways of mischief. In hindsight, only the tires are showing, revealing its tread, as are the steps of the mischievous one. Some think because they did not get caught right away in their misdeeds, they will not get caught, but in hindsight, they are found out.

Often people dress up and look distinguished to go out and impress others. But the one who will respect your efforts and appreciate you, whether you extend yourself or not, may be right next to you. Because people get caught up in the rhythm of the world, they allow the world to legitimize them by its standards. To be frank, they will never find fulfillment. The world is not designed to respect the sentiments of the heart but win at anyone's expense.

So, when you go searching for attention or love or are tempted to step outside your vows, remember: *Put not your trust in princes, nor in the son of man, in whom there is no help. His breath goeth forth, he returneth to his earth; in that very day, his thoughts perish* (Psalm 146:3-4). We are to trust in the Word of God and abide in Him.

And *Whoso findeth a wife findeth a good thing and obtaineth favour from the LORD* (Proverbs. 18:22). *A virtuous woman is a crown to her husband* (Proverbs 12:4a). These are powerful immovable precepts of God that lend favor to man. Obedience to His Word is life unto our bones. As well, they are provisions of assuredness that God is in control of everything.

We often spoil the freedom to choose by abusing its objective. There are rules in life that we should adhere to. There are also choices we make—substance builders—that allow one to stand in a matter to see its end. A husband that stands with his wife through adversity and obstacles that challenge their persons would rebirth a stronger love, even through the frustrations of life.

No matter how hard it may be, waking up to the truth will be another lesson learned. It is an increment to their being that blesses them in life into maturity, giving them more staying power.

For the first time in my life, I saw truly man. Because of my prejudice of the exterior, I was biased in my approach for my whole life. Until God showed him to me, I could not see because of my superficial way. I was introduced to him by a friend via email. When I saw from his picture that he was only fair-looking, I immediately rejected him and said, "I don't like him." However, in reality, I never knew him or gave him a chance to speak or even be.

I rejected him because I thought he wasn't good-looking enough. The Holy Spirit began to deal with my heart, and I realized I was wrong. I learned how shallow I was. We often reject people because of what they look like or what they have. We are not the master of their journey. Neither do we have our own completion. God knows what is best for us.

We have been brought up in a society that receives us by looks. I began to see the fruit of the spirit in this man. It was the God in Him that was most attractive and most important. Someone who loves God with their whole heart will also love you dearly. *"Those who have tied into great evidence have no crucial marriage."* This is true in Christ and in life.

We must understand that God stretches our faith by our belief in what He said He would do. We must also understand that character is built when we discern things unseen before in an individual. It is the intangibles of the spirit that completes them that bear good fruit. *"The wall doesn't know what the wall doesn't know."* The wall is the unknown, and we will not know what is on the other side unless we allow the experience. This is true in various facets of life.

For many reasons, people seek to impress others with their charades. In the end, they are spent emotionally and physically, and more times than not, financially. If being yourself does not get you where you want to be, maybe it is not where you need to be.

Individuals may strive to emulate what they see when they have not obtained the substance or what it takes to truly walk in those shoes. To them all, I urge, "Get Undressed."

Frequently we wear things to hide our inadequacies of anatomy. If we are too large, we wear black and avoid stripes. If we have a pudge or muffin top, we wear a bulky belt about our waist. We wear low heel shoes or high heels if we have a height complex, depending upon our disposition.

However, to become comfortable in our own skin and healthy from the inside out, we must get undressed. May we see ourselves for what and who we are. We begin by defining ourselves with the knowledge of understanding who we are in the Word of God. *Beloved, I wish above all things that thou mayest prosper and be in good health, even as thy soul prospereth* (2 John 1:2).

As we challenge ourselves, we know that *God hath not given us the spirit of fear; but of power, and of love and of a sound mind* (2 Timothy 1:7). To become the image we clearly want to partake, we must first get undressed. We must open the door to proper nutrition and exercise so that we may someday wear our clothes and stop allowing our clothes to wear us.

I joined the gym in 2003, and I have been getting in shape ever since. Getting in shape is a lifetime endeavor since we will be eating for a lifetime. I have never gone wrong attending the gym. When I was happy, it has proven successful. When I was sad, it has proven the same. No matter my state of mind, as I have gone through many journeys in life, I recall meditating and exercising through it all. It has been eighteen years, and I still find ways to get undressed and inspire stature and internal well-being. Being in shape will help you dribble the baseline, make a layup, or pass the ball. It will empower others to shoot the ball or perhaps see a need to get undressed to be more effective when it is game time.

It's better for a worthy subject to be waxed than for an unworthy subject to be waxed and cleaned. It is better to have substance than appear to have it. It is like building your house without foundation upon the earth. When the wind comes, it will be destroyed. When you keep His sayings and build your house upon the rock, a firm foundation, the winds may blow, but the house will continue to stand (Luke 6:48).

There may be times when a strange face comes through for you when the apparently familiar face will not budge on your behalf. This is not the time to become belligerent but understand the light of behavior. Your obvious choice may not be your best one.

We have to love ourselves. Equally important, do not define yourself by someone else's rules of life; find your own. Be sure that you are sold out to the right One. Sometimes people will prey upon your need in life to appeal to your personal interest. This is such an awful position for the opposed to possess. To have a brilliant mind and have found no cause to use it productively is demise. But instead, by manipulation, they prey upon the less fortunate to gain a greater wealth.

However this unfolds, the subject at hand was raised so that when they are older, they will not depart from their Godly upbringing. Therefore, at the grinding point of interacting and change, because of the fine line that separates the two, one is quickened by seeds planted long ago. They are seeds that say, "This isn't the will of God." Sometimes as we push through life, we find ourselves awakening from the sleep of successive days. Our experiences cause God's Word and many prayers to manifest in our days. When you realize how prevalent God is in your life, nothing can take that from you. You have been blessed by God.

There may be times when someone of great stature will put you in a situation where you are not prepared to complete the service. It is okay to let them know the job is not for you. Going through with it may end up hurting you and all those involved. It may be a feat that is out of your reach as you examine the situation. Never allow someone to overwhelm your poise by their demeanor and suggestions to the point you find yourself in a place that does not fit any of your strengths.

On the other hand, it is feasible not to assume what a situation entails in times of seeming despair. Your conclusion may end up off base and cause conflict to yourself and the entire gathering. To satisfy such an assumption may be harder to do than it would be to walk right in and allow the moment to speak for itself.

For example, there once was a man named Admer who walked away from a gathering. He assumed what one young lady had to say was not worth listening to. She began to speak on what seemed to be trivial things. She said, "I sure am thankful for waitresses, bus drivers, etc. I sure am thankful for them. If it wasn't for them, corporate America would miss out on the lower class partaking in big business growth, companies like Mr. Admer's that's growing leaps and bounds." Sometimes people forget about the majority who make it work. It is wise to hear the whole story before forming a conclusion.

Sharing moments with someone new may be entertaining and seem to be most fulfilling. In courtship, we find out right away if the relationship has staying power or not. People, unfortunately, can hide behind what looks decent and appealing until they are exposed. They would have you to be none the wiser. Looks do not always tell the whole story. But apple trees do not produce oranges, and we have the Word of God as our guide to try the spirits to see if they are good or evil (1 John 4:1).

Long ago, when sodas were four for a dollar, there was a kid who traveled along with other juveniles who plotted to make mischief. While he sat in the car with the getaway driver waiting for the others to come out of an abandoned warehouse, a car drove by them and circled the building. The kid known as the Baker kid got out of the vehicle. He was nervous and undecided. The driver motioned for him to get back inside, saying, "Don't worry, if they stop, I'll just tell them my name is Spencer instead of Charles. They won't think anything is wrong." The Baker kid did not buy it and slowly walked across the street to the local market. As he stood trying to appear normal, he pulled some change from his pocket along with some other coins that were of no significance. He began to count his change while looking around then at the orange-flavored soda in front of him. A little girl watched as he fumbled his change, trying to make sense of it.

Finally, the woman close to him gathered her things and went to purchase them. He had counted enough change for one soda pop, twenty-six cents to be exact. Meanwhile, things across the street had gone bad as he suspected they would. All seven of his friends were found trespassing and selling stolen goods. When news got back to town, the townspeople had them all in jail and accounted for and assumed the little Baker kid was also saying the worst stories imaginable. However, the little Baker kid made the right choice and chose not to be a part of the mischief. By the time the news reached Mrs. Baker, the little Baker kid had walked through the front door of their home. His mother shouted, "How could they? How could your sponsors be so irresponsible?"

Some may form opinions without knowing both sides of the story, giving a biased opinion. Even the courts will hear both sides of a story before delivering a verdict. However, when we make poor decisions and run with the wrong crowd, we may become guilty by association whether we get caught or not. Those who possess a position of authority are to lead by example. *Ever look at yourself in human bristle and grow beyond your last breath?* It is the moment that defines the next. That is what the little Baker kid did when he chose to leave his friends and go to the market.

Chapter 6

Positive Outcome of the Unknown

There are times when things are out of our control, and we must have faith in the Word of God. We are to stand on His promises regardless of how things look or appear to be. Because our hope is in Jesus, we give a supernatural response. We call those things that are not as though they were by faith because we choose to stand on His Word. Therefore, we believe in our hearts in the positive outcome of the unknown. We know that what we have petitioned God for is already done because of His finished work at Calvary.

Some say the body heals itself while we sleep. This reminds me of the Scripture, *For His anger endureth but a moment; in His favour is life: weeping endureth for a night, but joy cometh in the morning* (Psalm 30:5). I believe God sends events and opportunities to be a part of our own miracles through understanding the words of faith and perseverance. We must believe in the positive outcome of the unknown.

There once was a child who had a sickness the doctors couldn't cure, but there also was a woman who knew the illness the child had was a spirit she'd encountered. The woman was one of many that tried to cure this child. The woman went to the child one day and strangely began to reveal what had happened to her. She spoke to the spirit that had her bound. 'How unusual,' the child thought. Her approach was so different from the others. It seemed it might work. The child obeyed all that the woman said to do. As the woman spoke to the unidentified spirit, it began to move away from the child. As the child sat and began to talk, she noticed her voice was lighter, and she felt foreign from her adversity. It worked!

We all go through, some at the same time, but if we continue to fight, there's victory in the end. We may not see our way clearly at the time. Perseverance and faith will reveal your victory as you rejoice in how you overcame, appreciating those who war with you.

One day as I entered the YMCA where I work out, I was approached by the Athletic Coordinator with an idea to head up a girls' basketball program. The program was based on Christian ethics, building character, sportsmanlike conduct, and teamwork. I was said to be the perfect person for the job. Well, I could not have agreed more as my spirit referenced a passage in my earlier writings: *"There're times when someone else can stand, but when no one else can stand but you, answer the call."* I couldn't deny the truth. Therefore, I began mentoring girls ages twelve through seventeen years old through the Open Gym Basketball Program.

As my journey took flight, I began to realize the spiritual reason for this season. I was encouraged even more to fulfill God's purpose for my being there. I was sure my journey was not just about fundamental techniques in the game of basketball. One evening as I spoke to one of the parents, I realized the depth of the program. Before going to meet with the girls, I sat and pondered what drills to run. I also contemplated what to begin with for our second meeting.

It was quite strange because scheduling events did not flow like it did for our first meeting. I wondered why then I decided to trust God to lead me accordingly. After all, it was His seed that gave birth to my answering the call. As the girls gathered and our session began, we continuously moved on as time fulfilled the schedule. Near the end of our meeting, we gathered mid-court and sat in a circle where we shared our plans for the weekend and got to know one another better.

As we dispersed to go home, I knew how to proceed. Ultimately, everything we do should be for Kingdom building. I aimed to make sure the program edified the children by listening carefully and sharing and imparting God's wisdom into their lives as they sought a response. Always remember, do not break the covenant established between you and God when answering the call. The journey will go accordingly. Keep in mind why you are there from the start, and all will be rewarded. *Commit thy works unto the LORD, and thy thoughts shall be established* (Proverbs 16:3).

Tuesday, August 28, 2012 Goldsboro News-Argus — 7A

TODAY'S SNAPSHOT

A glimpse of life of Wayne County,

News-Argus/MICHAEL BETTS

Family YMCA instructor Pamela Young, left, gives a dribbling lesson to Jazlyn Grimes, 14, during the Girls Open Gym Basketball Program at the Family YMCA. According to Young, "The Girls Open Gym Basketball Program is based upon Christian ethics exemplifying teamwork, sportsmanlike conduct and building character." The program, which occurs every Tuesday and Friday from 5 to 7 p.m., is free to Family YMCA girls ages 12 to 17. Have something fun going on that would make a good snapshot? Call Michael Betts at 778-2211.

(From Goldsboro News Argus. Used by permission.)

In all that you do, put your best foot forward. Often, when we are put in a position to execute the *cause-gage* and answer the call immediately, we are on the other side. Then we trust God for our completion and to carry out the objective. Just as we have faith in the positive outcomes of the unknown, the enemy has planted seeds in the unknown. As we hear, things are happening around us but not to us; they are seeds of concepts. These are the realms of the unknown. While we have not experienced a thing, the enemy works in the spirit realm to enter the mind through seeds of our hearing. Our nature (flesh) grabs them and puts them to work, even without the enemy knowing; we sometimes initiate the fight.

For example: because we have a small inkling of what answering the call entails, our nature sometimes constitutes the worst scenarios possible. We become embattled until we realize if God is for us, then who can stand against us. There is a spiritual significance when answering the call, and we must understand the entire journey constitutes the same. Therefore, the way we answer the call in Christ is how we follow through.

As food for thought, consider these illustrations of life.

- How does the hand help someone else that is over you? He was compensated immensely for his work, but he was paid much more in heaven. His manual labor was incomparable to the seeds he sowed while he was there.

- An apple is like a smile that bears fruit. *A cheerful look brings joy to the heart, and good news gives health to the bones* (Proverbs 15:30 (NIV)).

- We modernize (conform) ourselves because we do not keep ourselves close to God.

- How can I go on without the basil? (Sometimes, we don't have all the ingredients for a recipe, but we use what we have.) Just go forward. Sometimes, we don't have everything we want or need in life, but it doesn't stop the day. We must press on and make the best of what we have, understanding the significance of the push.

- We will not smile outside the will of God. Everything we do is meaningless as a rocking chair rocks on.

- Choose your thoughts wisely, measure distance by the positive outcome.

- Sometimes when we lose things, it is so that we can find something we really need, as well as open the door for new possibilities.

- Consider your way and repent: *For we all have come short of the glory of God* (Romans 3:23).

The Lord is not slack concerning His promise, as some men count slackness, but is longsuffering to us-ward, not willing that any should perish, but that all should come to repentance (2 Peter 3:9).

38 Then Peter said unto them, Repent, and be baptized every one of you in the name of Jesus Christ for the remission of sins and ye shall receive the gift of the Holy Ghost. 39 For the promise is unto you, and to your children, and to all that are afar off, even as many as the LORD our God shall call. 40 And with many other words did he testify and exhort, saying, Save yourselves from this untoward generation. 41 Then they that gladly received his word were baptized: and the same day there were added unto them about three thousand souls (Acts 2:38-41).

- Hope imagines, as the doctor has said about the biopsy, that all is well.

- He spoke selectivity, *"Wherefore, my beloved brethren, let every man be swift to hear, slow to speak, slow to wrath"* (James 1:19).

- Some people with phones use backgrounds that are the imagination of loneliness. Often we mask our true feelings and replace them with other things such as conversations.

- There is always a new experience when we make a different choice. Be encouraged to try new things.

- Little Austin Maycoz preferred to play with girls rather than boys. No one knew his game but thought it quite strange. Surrounded by girls all the time, the boys teased his name. An onlooker saw a man behind a building waiting to rob a woman. Then suddenly, he went to her and began to speak. Just as the robber started to approach, he suddenly sought to retreat. A woman entered a courthouse and said she is tired and falls to her feet having a heart attack. A male juror races to her aid.

  Little Austin Maycoz has grown into a man who visited his friend one night and altered the devil's plan. As he continued to grow, there were seeds he must sow. On his last day of jury duty, he found another friend who lay on the floor with her life in his hands. Now Dr. Maycoz saved the life of his childhood friend. Every girl he encountered from his youth was part of God's plan, even the young lady he was in a relationship with. They would break up and make up; finally, he asked her to be his wife; she'd been his friend most of his life. Everyone plays a role in our lives, a perfect role. God has a purpose for everyone in your life; sometimes, it is to exit.

- When you have come from somewhere, don't allow anyone to take you back.

- Encouragement has no position and leaves out no one. We all are to edify one another in Jesus Christ.

- When you live by His Word, all things are possible; righteousness is power, and the enemy cannot touch you.

- Do not sell out even to yourself when only you know the compromise within.

- It is better to use thinking if you socialize it and examine its availability.

- Heaven is like the hem of His garment; as long as He is in the midst, all is well.

- Your efforts exceed your limitations without thought or contrast when you extend yourself to others, and home is lacking.

- When spirits agree, prayers go through.

- Do not die in your dreams; you are still alive. The day does not end when you go to sleep. There is still more to learn.

- The power of life is all that you are believing in, the manifestation of the unknown. It is His acquaintance with you before the foundation of the world through faith.

- Moving forward is acknowledging the totality of a situation.

- We covet our minds in the sanctuary of enablers, what best fits our shortcomings, so that we may not be rebuked, chastised, and found out. Thus, we are made aware and accountable for our actions and being; this should not be.

- The lessons we learn in life are substantial. Experiences give birth to God's sustaining power through our faith and perseverance in Him. It is a testament to others to look to Him in their most challenging times when humility is needed that bears great character. We receive strength no man can give, and no man can take away, as God molds us unto the day.

- I am the way I am; if I change one thing, I will not be the way I am. Because I thrive in a place does not mean I will succeed in another. I fit where I fit, not where others see fit.

Sometimes in life, we may have to run past those who assume to have the conclusion because the end is nowhere in sight. Making the best decision relies upon our spiritual integrity and not what seems to fit the purpose. Whereas the logical interpretation is omitted in efforts to oppose what is right and regard what looks right. The choices we really need to make are close to our hearts and will not lead us wrong.

Remember, a true leader leads no matter whose emotions are aroused to the left or the right. Whether it is a family member, friend, or others, the right of the truth is to prevail. Our perspective is to be pleasing in the eyesight of God.

- Others may try and fail but use what you know to the victories hail. Simply apply what is within, and you are sure to win, no matter what it looks like. That is the test that sanctions all to do their best. And when you stand in the midst of what seems to be chaos, remember where lay the key that unveils what you see on the other side of the controversy.

Ability tears down and rips apart what seems to need unscrewing. Will and desire pine away at sustaining structure and move matters to the other side and make the vision of its containment. Perseverance warms the chilled day with rays of the sun and cools the night with non forecasted weather. Whatever the task is, be sure to meet it. The invitation may not always be greetings, but the lessons you learn are worth the meeting.

- Be sure your hands are clean before the matter when you are sprayed with dirt; it will have no place to reside. Instead, it will be washed away. Your integrity becomes another's pride as you are called upon, selected, and favored above all others to do a job that is endeavored by many but who lack the heart for the task.

- It is an honor to bury a father in honor of God; a sword against lesser of it is futile.

- Will you exchange integrity and humility with someone who exemplifies neither?

- There are different interpretations of the bike.

  There once was a young lady who entered a cycling competition. She thought because she rode on a higher intensity level, she would win the tournament. However, there was another young lady whose ability to ride on a lower intensity level but at a faster pace was extraordinary. The other young lady could not believe she lost the event.

  Although this was true, her emotions did not deny her the victory. She was content with the effort she gave and wanted to know more of the strategies used at these games. She also admired the competitive company she was in. Good sportsmanlike conduct extends past the games we play and builds character inside and outside the sports arenas.

- Sometimes our lives dictate to us the paths we took only to reveal its last look. This Holy Counsel creates in us a clean heart and renews a right spirit within us (Psalm 51:10). So, understand and be established by God as He sets you apart.

- We have to give unclean spirits nowhere to land.

- The politics of the unknown is the real weather. No matter what, God is in control.

- Your capabilities are past your first impression.

- Once learning becomes understanding, then we begin enjoying the benefits of our labor.

- As layers of cheese reveal the softness of its textures, so do our experiences.

We look upon the outer surface, which appears strong and sturdy, but is soft to the touch. Sometimes we may feel weak, but our adversities reveal a stronger substance beneath us as we go through and find our strength through God. *And the God of all grace, who called you to His eternal glory in Christ, after you have suffered a little while, will Himself restore you and make you strong, firm, and steadfast* (1 Peter 5:10).

- Honor the Lord with the magnitude of your life.

- His disposition saved the animals. We never know when we will be needed because of the characteristics we possess.

- The right time is always being ready.

- If you never give up, you will always be ready.

- Stay committed to God; the best is yet to come.

Chapter 7

Walk in Greatness

Hanging on cords of despair to occupy a space may be time-consuming. Others may not remain in place to accomplish the task of the day. While some run to and fro to find their place, creating chaos, others are waiting to fill a position. Until you know where to properly go, keep your feet planted. There is no progress in ranting. While others may assume a role at their own discretion, it may be left up to another to make the correction. Everyone who stands in place or in your face is not where they are supposed to be, but where they are thought to be.

However, while this plays out, you may find yourself in a contingent apprehension. As subtle as it may be, this may cause others to view you in the same light—out of place. The extension of such a thing travels many ways. The objective is to be mindful of the company you keep and honorable so that it is productive. To linger in the discontent of others will permeate throughout the relationship. It can show proof and cause your growth to become halted and allude to your character. *The steps of a righteous man are ordered by the LORD: and he delighted in his way* (Psalm 37:23). Secure your walk building character without interference and guilty association.

On the other hand, there is the *showman,* someone you thought you had a good rapport with until a smart remark by an apparent stranger was made. Their demeanor became out of control and boisterous. You see behavior you detested but never saw before. As you both continued walking, trying to reach your destination, you try to encourage them otherwise. Still, they would not give it a rest. As you are passing others and certain individuals you know personally, still they are boisterous and use mannerisms you detest. Appalled and disgusted, you are approached by an acquaintance. They categorize and insult you because of the person you are with. You find yourself at a great impasse with the company you have kept and the disregard they have for others. You realize this mandates a change as you keep your poise. *Make no friendship with an angry man; and with a furious man thou shalt not go: Lest though learn his ways, and get a snare to thy soul* (Proverbs 22:24-25).

Sometimes people experience the most extensive hardship where even their family will stand together in an alliance against them, in situations where unwavering support is needed. Allow God's Word to be the peace that settles the storm and pierces the hardened hearts of even the ones closest to you. Because when the pendulum drops and tables turn the lesson, you saw then, they will have to learn or be subject to repetitive days and wayward ways. Stand on the Word of God and do not falter; cast your cares on God and leave them at the altar.

Similarly, teen reporters say mud, mayhem, and wonders have met. In the straight vision of their lives is played neglect. Adults with selfish desires and a fueling environment cater to uncomfortable associates. It invades all encounters of normalcy and comfort in homes. Their own counterparts are responsible and irresponsible, trying to live life on both sides of the fence. They indulge in sin and try to teach life lessons that do not comply and hit the floor because what is seen far outweighs integrity and respect but lose neglect.

Rage and malice, anger, and revenge play out before the eyes of little children and grown men, young adults, and their counterparts with little display of a kind heart. Even so, it does not fail to go unseen; when a child is covered and sheltered by another, their eyes gleam. It soothes their heart and grows their self-esteem. Amid it all, freedom rings.

- People who do not understand what God has done for them carry a heavyweight.

The enemy watches as you pass and go. Just as you are aware of the ebb and flow, God has given us a measure of understanding, and we must use it wisely. Do not allow your ego or flesh to dim your spiritual eyes. He appears as a compliment, his first strike, but you have seen him from a distance. Stay focused; don't choke. Resist him, and he will flee and have to revoke his charge. Wherein lay a life lesson from righteousness, where sin is realized. We should meditate on our deliverances, reference our journey, how God added a measure of understanding to our lives. May we not return to the vomit that is the taste of sin, a place where realization is a horrible place to stand. There is no pleasure there but detestation.

- The range of your thinking is not meant to detain you but take you further.

Remember, when seasons have ended, they have ended. The same attributes that brought you together in the first place may still be apparent. For that matter, they may always be there. However, the reason or reasons for separation or a new season is still apparent and meaningful. Do not be misled by emotions and mistake them for feelings that keep. It is a fine line, but it must be drawn.

Sometimes, we are sought out and remembered for attributes when another fails to exhibit them. I think the term often used is rebound. After the ball has been shot, other players scramble to get to it, even the shooter. After a relationship or friendship has ended, the same people revert because of a charismatic pull. They become reacquainted with a person to satisfy their need. So be diligent and recognize the smile, the conversation, and where you have journeyed from. Understand what is most conducive to growth in your life—building character and a fierce demeanor.

We must be led by God to deliver His Word. Sometimes the person you are talking to may not be in agreement with the Word delivered. However, it is meant to plant a seed that will begin to break the yoke intended by the Lord. Also, there are times when your spirit may be in one accord with theirs as you deliver a Word from the Lord, and it is received and confirmed. It does not mean because the person did not receive it that it was not the will of God. After planting a seed, it takes some time to grow.

We must establish a personal relationship with God. It is very important that we are led by Him.

My sheep hear my voice, and I know them, and they follow Me: And I give unto them eternal life; and they shall never perish, neither shall any man pluck them out of My hand (John 10: 27-28).

What you do now is preparing you for your season and will be significant for your future. So, do not faint. Stay the course; your season is coming. By wisdom, it will be received, and by understanding, it will establish you in the knowledge of the day.

Through wisdom is an house builded; and by understanding it is established: And by knowledge shall the chambers be filled with all precious and pleasant riches (Proverbs 24:3-4).

What is defined has its defining moments. There is more there than what you thought to be. The challenge is to be objective and examine its validity. Sometimes God allows us to revisit familiar places so we can see the totality of what was thought to be complete, an accomplishment only God can render in His perfection, a true life's lesson.

There are times when we look back and see more than we saw going forward. At first glance, things may appear to be okay, but seconds may reveal their actual setting. There was a young lady who was riding with a prominent basketball star. They passed some people she knew. The individuals were star-struck and smiled and waved as the car went by them. The looks on their faces were like kids on Christmas day. After they had passed, she and the star turned and looked back at them.

They saw the young lady's smile turn into a frown, and she was close to tears as the two young men with her overpowered the space between them. The car turned around, and the young professional athlete approached the men and demanded them to stand down, and the young lady was comforted. Unfortunately, this type of situation happens. Fortunately, someone was there to take a second look. As we are bound by the truth, we are freed by wisdom. May we apply the *preference zone* to our lives—muscles, math, integrity, etc.—anything that builds a person that we may truly appreciate one another.

Those closest to you can often pack a pretty mean punch, leaving an emotional scar, hurt, and sometimes anger. I once spoke with a dear friend who visited her in-laws. They treated her negatively in every aspect, although the relative she had come to see treated her kind. Agitated with their behavior, she began to exit the home when she heard a kind voice asking, "Where are you going? Are you coming back?" She replied, "Up the street to the store; I'll be back." As she drove to the store, she put in a CD and began to praise and worship God.

By the time she had returned to their home, she had realized her spirit was at peace. Praise and worship break the yoke of the unrighteous. When she entered the house, there were several exchanges from the kind one, and the others' demeanor seemed to be more inviting. She thought to herself how awesome prayer is and how important it is to go to a quiet place and worship the Lord in times of conflict. I realized a similar thing once after coming out of prayer. My mind was clear of everything, and there was oneness and peace so heavenly. I understood this peace is what God desires for me and that if anything began to alter it, it has to go. And I have a sure way of getting to this place in prayer.

It is better to give than to receive. One morning, I woke up, looked towards the blinds, saw the light of day, and thought, "I made it to see another day," and was very thankful. As I opened the blinds, I saw that it was raining and remembered my mother, who had a meeting to attend, does not like to drive in the rain. So, I hurried and got dressed to accompany her. By the time I was ready to exit my home, the rain had stopped.

I went to say good morning to her anyway. She asked, "Why are you dressed up?" I replied, "I was going to drive you to your meeting." We both looked at each other and smiled. I visited for a few minutes and returned home. I undressed and hung my clothes in the closet, but not before trying on another jacket and some pants. Before long, I was organizing my closet. I thought, wow, the extension of giving certainly gives back to you.

Sometimes people may call something other than what it is to get you there. Identify it and capitalize on the moment. For example, a man was visiting his alma mater; he pulled out a pendant that represented the college basketball team. When asked why he did that, he said so all would know that it was his alma mater and he once played sports there. As he mingled and conversed with others, he realized a young lady seemed to be uncomfortable. He comforted her by making himself an obstacle and the brunt of his jokes. She lightened up and began to smile. When another of the visitors had a problem with their car later that evening, he went to get gas to help them along the way. Even though this young man was manipulated into going to this event, his disposition was capitalized upon, and his presence was greatly needed. Gaining is to be discerning as to mirror the gospel character and be concerned as every Christian should.

Even though your heart may be in the right place concerning another as you exercise the *preference zone,* another may not be receptive at first. Plant the seed anyway. As subtle as it may seem, through faith, growth is apparent. The apparatus needed to sow into their lives will reap a harvest in due season, and God's will be done.

- *On-the-job training* is listening to someone when no one else is there to listen. It is reiterating in a moment's time to learn a line capitalizing on the moment. Or eating an apple until you can have a full course meal. The lessons we learn in life require work.

Because you have not seen someone does not mean they are not looking for you. When you acknowledge them, it may be the end of their search, as well as penance for their absence. Everyone should not be labeled the same even though the situation seems similar; accredit the duration of the journey until it has passed. Wait to see what the end entails.

- Be a doer!

In this year, we will begin a walk in greatness, where we no longer allow our flesh to lead, but it is an apparatus that we arrive and do the will of the Lord. There comes a time when you have been called, and there is no other choice but to do His will. It is in your bones, and you have been established in Him. When we understand and begin to walk in the Spirit and are led into the unknown, there is a oneness and depth to life that inspires us to submit to His will. A place of revelation has you dressed and prepared for an event yet to come as our heavenly Father prepares the finishing touch. We are going somewhere. We must first surrender and give our lives to Him so that we may begin a walk in greatness.

Without the skin, there'll be a lot of other exchanges in the base. For example, having a cold, infection, bruising, and inability to heal properly can come from having a lowered immune system. We are designed for the purpose of prosperity and longevity among sorts and a union to enable one another in this effort. Humanity is a creation far beyond reach or design and will never be equaled. It is God's will that our souls are saved so that we may live again. So, as we journey through life with a conscious mind, may we acknowledge the design, appreciate our capabilities, and honor the temple that houses the soul. May we prefer the Word of God that the Creator gave to promote life in both spiritual and physical aspects. May we walk in greatness as we partake inwardly and outwardly of the gospel character reverencing God and Scripture.

Speak and make known the Word of God in your life so that others may hear and listen to kindred spirits while we reign on earth.

"Your life trial is your field of dreams."
(Holy Spirit).

About the Author

Pamela M. Young, a native of Goldsboro, North Carolina, is a professional poet. She is the daughter of Mrs. Edna M. Young and the late Mr. William Alexander Mitchell, Sr. After high school, she continued her education at Norfolk State University, later studying at Mt. Olive College.

Her original works are sold at Hallmark, A Mustard Seed, and Christian supply stores. She is the author of *Stand: An Autobiography of Poems* and *A Poet's Decree: Rhythm of Life*. She has had guest appearances on local television in her area and is a member of The Speakeasy Project (Documentaries of Poets). She encourages growth and a positive outlook on life by reciting poems to the youth in her community.

Pamela M. Young

Breath of a Poet

Other Books by Pamela M. Young

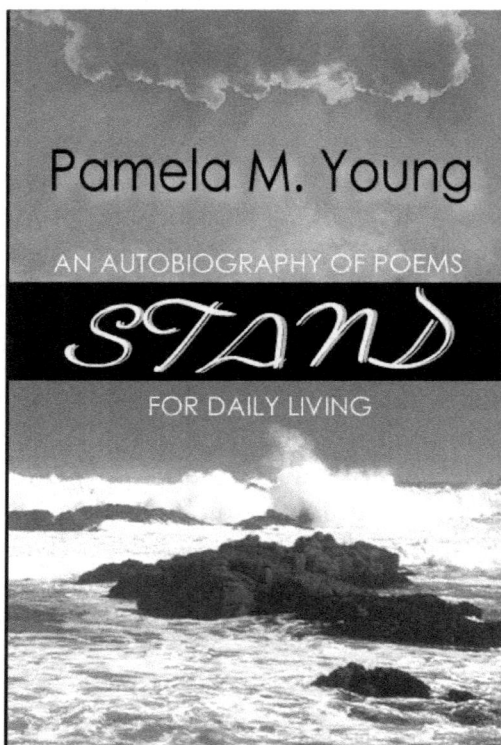

Pamela M. Young

AN AUTOBIOGRAPHY OF POEMS

STAND

FOR DAILY LIVING

(ISBN: 978-0-9799798-2-8)

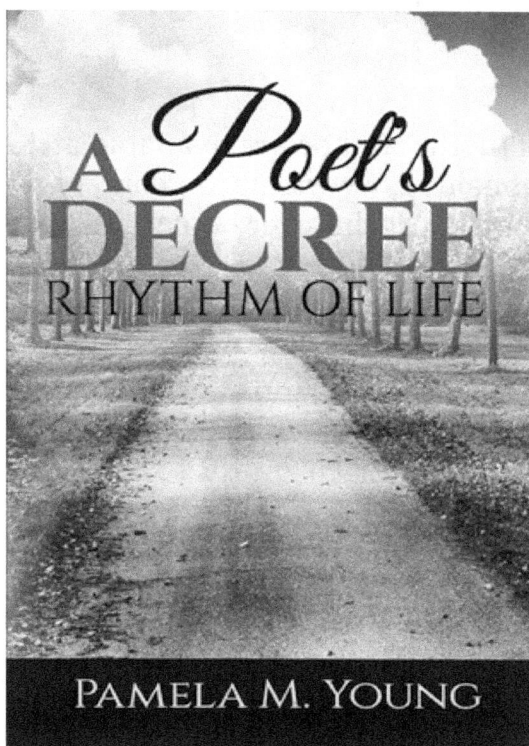

A Poet's
DECREE
RHYTHM OF LIFE

PAMELA M. YOUNG

(ISBN: 978-0-9968089-1-0)

Contact Information

All books by the author are available at Kingdom Living Publishing, www.amazon.com, www.barnes andnoble.com, or wherever books are sold.

Kingdom Living Publishing
P.O. Box 660
Accokeek, MD 20607
publish@kingdomlivingbooks.com
301-275-9014